michael jans'
INSURANCE
PROFIT
SYSTEMS

The P & C
Marketing Bible

13 Amazing Agents Reveal Secrets on How To Dominate Your Marketplace

By Michael Jans

"Dare I say that these 13 are the disciples? Michael Jans has truly developed a system that changes the insurance game. As an entrepreneur starting a new agency from absolutely nothing, I'm excited to learn from amazing agents that are successful and are doing it right. If all you want to be is a typical insurance agent, don't read this book and just keep doing the same old stuff. Many thanks to Michael and the 13 in this book for sharing what has made you successful!"

Tom Davenport
Blue Marsh Insurance, Inc.
Birdsboro, PA

"Prior to responding to Michael Jans' invitation to join Quantum Club I had found myself "stuck in a rut", bored with my business, overwhelmed with monotony, and incapable of imagining a better future. That all changed rapidly as I got involved in Quantum Club. Now I'm overwhelmed with new ideas and possibilities. The camaraderie and support I receive from other members has been a tremendous encouragement when I come up against some of the challenges of running a business. The tools that are provided to us are invaluable aids to analyzing where we are at, where we need to go, and how to get there. I joined Quantum Club to address just one aspect of my business. What I received in return was a comprehensive network of tools, trainers, and encouragers dedicated to helping me improve not just my business....but my life."

Jerry Brewton, CLU, ChFC, CIC
Brewton Insurance Protection Team
Elkhart/Goshen/Noblesville, IN

Dedication

This book is dedicated to my father, Paul Jans. As the first white student to attend the "all Negro college" of Howard University, he showed me the power of doing precisely the opposite of what everyone else does. As the founder of Meals on Wheels in the United States, he showed me the force of a good idea and the power of community to change the world.

To my mother, June Jans, who intuitively knew what we all seek to know: that we're all made of the same stuff. From her, I got the rare but precious glimpse of the profound significance of that fact.

To my children, Rachel, Maggie, Lucas, Jacob and Adrian, who continue to teach me most of what matters.

To my wife, Teresa, who taught me that love is constant, and joy is its steady companion.

Preface

I have been an agent in the Insurance Industry for over 16 years. I have been blessed in business for 2 reasons: #1 I have a contract with the best damn insurance company in the world, and #2 I have known Michael Jans for 14 years!

From his simple Unique Selling Proposition (USP) – More Control, More Money, and More Time Off – to his P&C Profit Circle and every tool in between – Michael brings more value than all the Coaches/Consultants that have ever tried to help the Insurance Agent!!

This book is not only a must read for every insurance agent but also for any business person, practitioner, business major, or MBA Graduate that is serious about growing their business with less stress. Michael does not teach theory – he teaches real life business principles that can be applied to any business practice.

You will use this book as a reference for years to come – have a highlighter ready, take notes, and dog ear the pages; you are getting ready to learn from one of the best – the "Bad Boy" of the Insurance Industry!

James Brown
September 2008

Forward

Back in the late 1960's, political radical Abbie Hoffman wrote a book called, "Steal This Book." I was tempted to deliver an equally contrarian piece of advice and call this one **"Don't read this book"**. At least that's what I would tell most insurance agents. Why?

Because it seems that most agents are happy with *average agencies*. Most are happy with *average lifestyles*. Most are happy *working too many hours*. Most are happy *making far less money than they could*. And, sadly, most are happy – or shall we say satisfied – proving to their families that they can only achieve so much and only provide so much.

In my decades-long career as coach and consultant to thousands of P&C agents and agency principals, I'm well aware that less than one in a 100 agents will respond to my "call to arms." The vast majority of souls are complacent and remain blissful in their ignorance; a handful will listen in a bizarre information-gathering exercise never to take the first step, while fewer still will listen, implement, and reap the benefits. Sadly, this is not unique to the industry – it's human nature.

And while it's easy to complain about the pressures on the industry – and they are out there as immense

9

as a den bear – far too many cower in the corner, quaking at the perils of the changing market, shivering at the menace of the mass marketers, shuddering at the threats of alternative distribution systems, the internet, and disloyal carriers. And far too many agents secretly gripe about producers who don't produce and CSR's who don't close the inbound calls or cross sell their existing customers.

All that complaining and griping will take its natural course...to nowhere. In the meantime, for many agents – these pressures *will* slowly pilfer their income, forcing them to hustle for business while clients quietly sneak out the back door – leading to exhaustion, fatigue and burnout.

And while these agents – virtually all good people and important members of their community – publicly declare their love of family and belief in "The American Way," they continually prove otherwise by settling for average income, vulnerable businesses, squeezing pennies from one-at-a-time sales and bouncing along on creaky, wobbly business systems.

And for those who are A-Okay with business-as-usual, my recommendation, again, **don't read this book.** It will only make you mad – most likely at yourself. And that never helped anyone.

But for those agents who are dead serious about making a difference for the people who rely on them – family, clients, staff – and who want the best for themselves, I reverse that directive and urge you to *read this book*. For those who dream that someday they may "live the dream," those who would like to know what it's like to "pinch yourself to see if it's real," those who truly want to own and run a world class agency and enjoy the perks that go along with that and those who simply want to look at their life and their business with the pride of accomplishment, I *implore* you - *read this book.*

Why? *Not* because I wrote it. On the contrary - for the most part - I really *didn't* write it. This book was "written" by the real-life stories of 13 outstanding agents. Each of them chose to look at this business a little differently. Each of them *chose* to believe that the impossible was possible:

- <u>That they no longer had to chase clients</u>; rather, they chose to believe that clients would *chase them*. And they set up systems to make that happen.

- <u>That business did not have to get harder and more complicated to run when it got bigger</u>; rather, they chose to believe that it can be simpler and more satisfying. And they set up systems to make that happen.

- <u>That they don't have to work longer hours to make more money</u>; rather, they chose to believe they can work fewer hours and take more vacations. And they set up systems to make that happen.

- <u>That the demands of running an agency do not need to burn you out.</u> Rather, they chose to believe that business can be increasingly fun and personally fulfilling. And they set up systems to make that happen.

And each of them – without exception – has begun to see those beliefs become reality. Each is making more money...taking more time off ...and having more fun.

So the reason I urge you to read this book is because it is the narrative of achievement, told in the actions and subsequent results in the real world by 13 remarkable agents - all of them *just like you*.

From time to time, some of my clients accuse me of being almost "militant" in my message. I'll take that as meaning that they perceive me as being "passionately stern". And I take it as a compliment.

The times they are a-changin'. Many of the threats that agents perceive today <u>are</u> real. I've been in this industry long enough to see many, many good agents get side-swiped by the pressures and challenges of an unpredictable economy and a maturing industry. Now is <u>not</u> the time for agents to hide their heads in the sand. We've seen market cycles "thin the herd" of agents before. Tens of thousands of agencies that existed a few decades ago are gone, gone, gone. That process will continue –and, very likely, the new pressures of e-commerce, global economic turmoil and alternative providers will *accelerate* the process.

One last point. In the following pages, you are going to meet 13 agents who have undergone a process of transformation. For the uninitiated, this process may seem intimidating. You may be tempted to think of 1000 reasons why "your agency is different" and somehow you don't qualify to join in the fun. Don't give in to that temptation.

While the process may seem intimidating, the payoff is huge. I know that for two reasons. I've seen it with hundreds and hundreds of agents who have followed the same steps these agents took.

They have found that the process is NOT intimidating. It's invigorating. It's fulfilling. And it has made them a lot of money.

I still remember the day when I thought my agency was a millstone around my neck – stealing my time, my freedom and giving me little in return. But I got lucky. I found someone who shined a light for me and revealed the secrets to rapid business growth and financial freedom.

I hope that I – and these 13 agents – can do the same for you.

Michael Jans

Contents

Part One –
Michael Jans:
The Man,
The Vision

The purpose of this
book is simple. To give
you a roadmap to
success for your
agency. Clearly, the
book is not for
everyone. It's for the
principals of property & casualty agencies. If that's
not you, this book isn't for you.

I hope to accomplish two things in order to achieve
my purpose. The first is to *change your mind.*
Literally, *change* the way you think. That's because –
as each of my 12 featured agents will attest – the first
and most important change is a *change of mindset.*

Most agency principals think of themselves as agents.
I want to encourage you to think of yourself as a
marketer who happens to be in the insurance
business. *Because marketers are in the business of
growing the business.*

Marketers are in the business of attracting, converting
and keeping customers at the highest possible long-
term profit. If you own the business, this is your

responsibility. Nobody else will do it for you. Nor *should* they.

Of course, you need good technical skills in the agency. Without those technical skills, you'll have a hard time growing fast or keeping your clients. Yet far too many agency principals *only* think of themselves as technicians – *BIG mistake.*

Without customers, your technical skills are useless. The fundamental responsibility of the owner is profitably acquiring and subsequently keeping customers. When you go from accepting – to embracing – and finally, *living out* this responsibility in your business, the rewards are astronomical.

The second thing I want to accomplish to achieve my purpose is to give you a blueprint. And rather than simply *tell* you how to do it, I felt it would be more powerful and more beneficial for you if I *show* you. That's why I decided to feature real-world, in-the-trenches stories of other agents – those who have already executed some of the strategies I teach my members and clients.

Once a month, I conduct a live teleconference for our Quantum Club Members where I interview a very successful client, and they share many of the marketing and business secrets that have worked well for them. Not more than 24 hours before the time of this writing, I interviewed one of the featured agents in this book, Gordon Sorrell. At the end of the call, he said to the agents who were listening, "I can't emphasize enough, pay attention to these tools and put them to use. **They'll make you a millionaire.**"

That, in fact, is my PROMISE to you. Put the tools we talk about in this book to use, *and they will make you a millionaire* - many times over.

In fact, that's exactly what happened to me. But there was certainly a time in my life when I was NOT a millionaire - far from it...

A Stranger in the Park Changes My Life Forever

This story may strike you as odd or unusual. The circumstances were, indeed, unusual for me, and, as you will see, changed my life forever.

Many years ago, I ran an insurance agency. During my early period in that business, times were tough as nails. One day, in despair, I strolled from my office to spend some time alone. I sat next to an old man on one of the green benches under the large oak trees in the park. He was well dressed, but otherwise non-descript.

We both sat quietly on the bench for a few minutes, pondering our own private thoughts. "You've had better days," he flatly observed.

That felt like a slap in the face. My skin bristled on the

defense against this complete stranger. I prepared to leave, but as I glanced back, I was surprised to see a face as welcoming as an open fire that somehow beckoned for me to unload my burden on him. Before I knew what was happening, my story tumbled out of me.

At the time I had four children. I was working more than sixty hours a week, yet business was still rotten. The future seemed bleak. I longed for the simple, early days of my marriage, when I could enjoy spending free time with my wife and kids. But now I felt imprisoned by circumstances, certain I would never return to such innocent times.

I explained to him that although I did have a lot of friends in the industry, and I was trying to learn from them as quickly as I could – it just wasn't happening fast enough.

The Old Man broke into my sob story and interjected, "No wonder you're having problems". Unless you want to be like everyone else in the industry, why would you go to them? Don't settle for being average, or even for being above average."

I was confused. Maybe I expected something more like a Mr. Rogers response. But what I got was like a stern talking-to from my high school basketball coach. Either way, I grew irritated. Clearly, I was wasting my time.

"You'll excuse me" said the stranger, "but I have an obligation. An old friend is not well, and I promised to pay him a visit."

"Have a nice day," I said, anxious to be alone again.

"But, if you'd be willing to meet me here tomorrow at the same time, I think I could solve your problem. In fact, I think I could make you a very wealthy man."

No sooner than I found myself barely able to resist laughing in the old man's face, a black stretch Jaguar limousine eased up to the curb.

He said, "Here's my driver. Perhaps I'll see you tomorrow." I thought I caught a smirk as he tipped his hat and ambled off toward his car. As the limo disappeared into the distance, I sat there slack-jawed, wondering *whom* I had just encountered.

That evening, I told my wife about my bizarre encounter. "All you've been talking about is how hard things are at work. Why don't you go see him tomorrow? Besides, what have you got to lose?" She was right. At this point, I was open to suggestions – even those from a strange (but apparently rich) old man.

The following morning at the agency, my concentration wandered. As much as I tried to convince myself that going to the park to see an old stranger was a waste of time, when the time came, I found myself walking toward the park – with a quickening pace.

His warm smile instantly put me at ease, as if he sensed my doubts. "Let me make something perfectly clear. I won't give you a penny. I won't offer you a job. But, I will give you something much more valuable, and, if you put my advice to work, you *will* become a wealthy man. And, you will have the time you seek to spend with your family. You should also know, I know nothing about insurance. I hope that doesn't disappoint you."

"So...*are you interested?*"

Before I had the chance to shift the conversation and ask him who he was, he began to pepper me with questions. His eyes twinkled with interest at my answers...and lack thereof.

"Can you explain your marketing model? How do you generate leads? How do you convert your leads? How much do you pay for leads? How much is your cost per sale? How much are you willing to pay for new business? What's your most profitable line of business? What's your best up-sell strategy? How do you retain your clients? Can you explain your client segmentation process? What marketing strategies are you testing in your business right now?" His questions came at me relentlessly. I felt like the sparring partner of an old boxing pro, fast on his feet with moves I'd never seen. I stammered out my answers, dizzy with confusion. But he was persistent with his questions.

"What's your experience with multi-step sequencing? Who writes your marketing copy? What do you do with unconverted leads? Who are your joint venture partners? Can you explain how your best referrals strategies work? How do you select your niche markets? What's the lifetime value of your average customer? Of your VIP's? How do you compute Total Customer Value? Best of all, tell me about some of your marketing tests that failed and what knowledge you gained from them?"

I felt like a fool.

"Don't be embarrassed," he said, seeing my discomfort. "I'm simply gathering information." "I've never even thought about most of these questions. And the ones I have thought about, I don't have good answers for."

"Do you think you'd like to work with me?"

"I'm desperate," I reminded him. "I'll try anything."

A smile broke across his face. "I'll take that as the compliment of a desperate man, then. And perhaps I'll see you here tomorrow."

Just then, his limousine slid up to the curb. "Please excuse me. I have an ill friend I must go see. I hope you have a wonderful day," he said, as he headed to the car.

Of course, I did see him the next day...and the next - and so on, for the next three months. We spent hours and hours together, engaged in conversations that sped by like minutes. I furiously filled notebooks with ideas, strategies and insights, and he was even kind enough to draw charts and diagrams of marketing models.

To this day, I go back to those early notes for inspiration and "ideas I forgot I knew." Invariably, they are as fresh as the day the ink dried on the paper, each page bursting with easy ways to make money.

On a few precious weekends, my new friend joined my wife and me as we took our children to the zoo or the park. "No business," he commanded. "This is family time." My children enjoyed his warm personality. I think he enjoyed them even more.

During the course of those three months, he unraveled the mysteries of marketing and business for me. I learned secrets that really did change my life forever.

It wasn't long at all before I chopped my hours down to an acceptable forty. My business was growing.

Prospects were calling us. Money was starting to roll in. Staff morale was at an all time high. And I was spending time with my family again.

It wasn't long before many of my friends in the industry began to notice the outward signs of my success: a new house, a new car. Our staff grew quickly to meet the demand of our expanding customer base. I wanted to share my secret with them. When I saw my "marketing wizard" at the park, I asked him if he'd be willing to meet with other agents and teach them the way he was teaching me.

"My public days are over. But, when you are ready, then *you* can share your knowledge with them. But, Michael, I'd just as soon you keep my name out of the limelight."

"Then I'll call you my 'Deep Throat,'" I joked, "Because you tell the truth but don't want anyone to know it's coming from you" (Little did I know that his amazing nuggets of truth would eventually knock an entire industry on its backside, in true "Deep Throat" tradition).

The very next day, when I went to the park, my friend wasn't there. I was surprised, and a little hurt. I thought, "He should've called. He's never done this before."

That night, after dinner, the phone rang. My wife

answered "Yes, yes, I understand. I'm so sorry. I'll tell him right away. Thank you."

"I'll drive you to the hospital," she said, as she shot me a look full of meaning. "He wants to see you right now."

"The hospital? What happened?"

"His daughter just said he was hoping he could see you, and he thought it should be tonight."

As I walked down the hospital corridor, I came upon a swarm of people. The waiting room was jammed.

"You must be Mr. Jans. I'm his daughter. He's spoken quite a bit about you. Would you mind seeing him now?"

"Of course not," I said, as she led me to his room. His face was pale, but his eyes still twinkled. His hand felt cold as he squeezed my own hand tightly. I did my best to swallow back my emotions, but with little success.

"Well, Michael, I suspect we've had the last of our little conversations."

"The last! How can that be?" I exclaimed, grinning the toothy grin of denial, all the time my eyes acknowledging the inevitable.

Undeterred, he uttered, "Michael, I've had a wonderful life, but I'm an old, sick man. And, as you know, I've made an awful lot of money. That's been fun. It's allowed me a tremendous amount of freedom, and given me the joy of exploring the world in ways I never dreamed of as a child."

"It's provided opportunities for my family that have been a delight for all of us. But, please remember this - the greatest joy of all is not the money. It's them," he said, as he gestured in the direction of the hospital waiting room, crammed with family and friends.

After we spoke for a few minutes, I said "Perhaps I should leave you to your family."

His gaze went through me. "Michael," he said.

"Yes, my friend."
"You know what this means, don't you?"

"Um...well, I'm not sure."

"It means *now it's your turn*."

I stared at him intently, unsure of his meaning.

"To teach the secrets! To wave the wand of freedom...to show the way to the fullest life on earth...to grant the dream upon which this great country was born."

"...But I'm not ready," I protested.

He cut me off mid-sentence "Please, no excuses. All I ask is this. If what I've told you is true, *share it*."

Silence hung in the air between us like a third presence in the room.

"But...in the end, it's up to you."

"You can count on me," I promised, the words echoing loudly in my head as I realized I had just made a promise to a man on his death bed.

Three days later I was shocked to see over a thousand people at his funeral. Somehow, I felt he had been "my" secret, but I couldn't have been more wrong. It was clear that he had touched many lives during his time on this earth.

As I headed toward my car, his daughter ran from the church, calling my name. "He told me," she said. "I'm pleased for you."

"Told you what?" I asked.

At that moment, someone called her name. "I'm so sorry. I really should head back. Good luck to you.

I'm sure you'll do well."

"..But what did he...?" Too late. She was well on her way.

I was left to ponder what he had told her. But I suspected I knew. I felt myself protesting against it like a child at naptime. The burden was more than I wanted.

All these years later, as I reflect upon my own success, I am reminded of my promise, that he could "count on me." Never in my wildest dreams, did I ever imagine I would make so much money. Never did I think I would accumulate this much wealth. And never, did I think that it would be possible with so little effort. Overall, my deepest satisfaction has been the ability to give my family so many opportunities.

All this, I owe to the secrets revealed to me by my "Deep Throat". In fact, his original insights set me upon a path to discovering secrets and strategies that he probably could not have taught me - insights I suspect he never knew.

Since then, I have sought out the best of mentors, traded secrets with friends and colleagues, and devoured every proven technique I could get my hands on. Above all, he taught me to be a serious student of marketing and business, and I believe he would be proud.

28

What I Learned That Day In The Park

Fifteen years ago, prior to that fateful day in the park when I met my first mentor, I was in a desperate situation. I had taken over an insurance agency on the brink of collapse. I was spending too many hours away from my large family, frantically trying to save the company from bankruptcy - yet what I was doing was clearly NOT working.

What was I doing wrong? I wrung my hands in frustration, certain I had done everything possible to make the agency profitable, yet nothing worked. Surely the stars were aligned against me. After all, I had been carefully modeling my business approach after the techniques of other insurance agencies...yet I didn't seem to have the results I *assumed* they were enjoying.

I had looked to the industry experts for answers. Yet it was my friend on the park bench that day who revealed that was my *biggest mistake*. He showed me how although the agencies that I had considered exemplary were technically correct in their business plans, they were "circling the wagons", as it were - essentially only looking to *themselves* for guidance. And here I was, caught in the same circle - where the view never changes.

He explained to me that basic marketing skills can only take a business so far. If I wanted to excel outside of the "circle of wagons" I had to start thinking differently about marketing. It was simply *impossible* to market the same way as others and expect a different result. And I needed more than average results to get myself out of the quagmire I was in. I needed *BIG* results, trust me.

The marketing systems he showed me were completely different than what was the "norm" in the industry. In fact, they were vastly different from 99% of businesses around the world! They focused on building client relationships, increasing long-term customer value, and most of all – increasing profits.

Most importantly, he explained how to set up my marketing, a world-class team, and have every aspect of my company run on autopilot. He showed me that my business was not a "job" - I needed to know how to make my business work for me. When and *only* when I did this – according to the old man in the park - would I begin enjoying higher income while working fewer and fewer hours.

The impetus was on me to take action, so I started with a simple postcard. Just months before, a colleague had created a postcard for me which resulted in one measly lead. That was enough to get me thinking... using my newfound knowledge, could I improve the response?

So I designed my own postcard – the result? The campaign generated a staggering *118 leads.* I felt like a god! It was like having my very own customer faucet that I could turn off and on at will.

As a result, I threw out all conventional business plans and started implementing strategies that would eventually go on to totally change the landscape of insurance marketing. I devised creative, effective techniques that immediately boosted my profits and turned my agency around.

People took notice. My groundbreaking system began drawing the attention of fellow insurance agents, some of whom would openly call me and ask me what I was doing. It was becoming apparent that I had broken away from the "circle of wagons". While some were quick to (predictably) criticize something they clearly didn't understand, others practically begged me to share my newfound secrets, and take me with them.

And as any good "convert" should be, I found that I was eager to share my new "faith" with anyone who showed an eagerness to learn. I soon discovered I had a passion for teaching, especially when my students went on to follow my advice and profited from it. Nothing thrilled me more than hearing their excited voices on the other line saying things like "Honestly, Michael, I didn't believe it would work, but we tried it anyway, and I just can't believe the response! *It's amazing!"*

My first mentor must have seen this fire in me, even before I knew it was there. Perhaps in his wisdom, he knew that the seemingly *staggering* deathbed request he had made of me was my life's calling anyway. Perhaps it wasn't so staggering after all.

The result was a natural progression from focusing solely on my own personal success - to educating others to follow my lead, resulting in the founding of Insurance Profit Systems, Inc. And I can unabashedly claim that Insurance Profit Systems, Inc. is now the saving grace of the struggling insurance industry. How can I be so bold? That part comes easy for me.

In fact, I have been called a maverick, a renegade, a bad boy, a rebel and an iconoclast, you name it. In fact, I wear it as badge of honor. This industry *needs* shaking up now more than ever. Insurance agents have never faced greater obstacles to success: commission cuts, a soft market, fickle carriers, and never-before-seen competition are resulting in a frenzy of mergers and acquisitions – accompanied by massive lay-offs. Good agents are being forced out of business every day, losing their incomes and devastating their retirements.

However, MY agents will weather the storm with flags flying. Bottom line - my clients make more money.

Why? Because they *know* more than other agents. Frankly, my clients will thrive at the expense of the ignorance of others, as they use their know-how to steal customers from the uninformed. In fact, more than 1,600 insurance agents have joined forces with IPS to market their way into a high-profit, high-income future - and our numbers grow daily.

The Amazing Agents

The stories you are about to read come from my best of the best. These are agents with marketing strategies and sales goals that *blow away* the average agent. These are outside of the box thinkers, mold-breakers, and leaders in this industry.

They were chosen from hundreds of submissions for our annual Best Year Ever Contest. Besides getting our attention with outstanding success stories, the finalists you'll meet in this book all demonstrated excellence in the following areas:

Financial Growth. Top and bottom-line growth was tracked in three dimensions: new clients, revenue per client, and client retention. These agents are experts in "smart marketing." Luck was <u>not</u> involved!

Auto-Pilot Strategies. The Dirty Dozen have set the standard for auto-pilot "Robot Marketing", meaning their agencies run smoothly, even when they're out of the office.

Industry Leadership and "Quantum Citizenship."
Community is as important to this industry as
leadership. These agents are mutually dedicated to
the common successes and mastery of other
members. They are willing to share ideas, volunteer
support for fellow members, and demonstrate the
highest level of commitment to the insurance
community.

Quality of Life. Perhaps most importantly, these
finalists have used Insurance Profit Systems'
techniques to create a deeply satisfying life. Their
compelling stories are examples to all agents who
want to improve their businesses, and live out the life
of their dreams.

Get ready to meet the men and women who exemplify
excellence in insurance, leadership, and most
importantly - in life! As a result of their own
experiences and triumphs, these agents can pass
down the life-altering power of IPS and Quantum Club
better than anyone. So without any further ado, I'd like
to introduce you to the Dirty Dozen!!

Part Two – Conversations with the Dirty Dozen

1 – Claudia McClain

THE DIRTY DOZEN DIARIES

"It is my respected peer group that challenges me, by their example and their mentoring, to greater success than I could ever have imagined."

-CLAUDIA MCCLAIN

Claudia McClain is the daughter of a stock broker, so she spent her middle and high school years working for her father, doing any type of boring clerical task he needed accomplished. This exposure to wealth management and risk and commissioned sales taught Claudia the value of a career that financially rewards you for working intelligently and strategically.

While attending college, Claudia worked in the management training program for Sears. After managing the Fabric & Yarn department in a local Sears store, she was promoted to Catalog Sales Trainer for the Los Angeles region. Claudia's introduction to retention and cross-selling strategies came at age 22, when her primary responsibility was to teach telephone sales clerks in each of the 110 southern California catalog departments and neighborhood appliance stores how to cross sell and up sell. "Our detergent is on sale. Shall I add a box to your order?"

In 1976, Claudia re-evaluated opportunities at Sears and realized that there were careers where she could write her own paycheck through hard work and creativity. She returned to the financial services field, this time as a life agent for Metropolitan Life. Later that year, her soon-to-be husband asked the magic words, "Do you like rain?", and they headed north to Everett, Washington so he could pursue a career opportunity.

Newly married and not knowing a soul in the great Northwest, Claudia decided to change tracks and consider the property/casualty side of the insurance house. She was referred to a small regional carrier, PEMCO Mutual Insurance. PEMCO was one of the first companies to have a "dual marketing system." The company sold half of its business through independent agents and half through the "house," keeping operational costs and premiums low. Claudia had the opportunity to build her own agency, one client at a time. She sold

PEMCO "house accounts" during the day, and solicited her own accounts at night and on weekends.

In 1980, Claudia left PEMCO and established her own very small personal lines agency in her home in Everett, which was 30 miles north of Seattle. The agency grew gradually as her son, and then daughter, joined the family. By the time the children were in school, Claudia had relocated the agency to an office location - with a room in the back for the kids to do homework while Mom worked.

Claudia is most inspired by, and most proud of, her successful family, which includes Pat, her husband of 31 years, her son Tim, age 29, and daughter Caitlin, age 25.

The entrepreneurial spirit runs deep in the family. Claudia's youngest brother, Kirk, owns two large bakeries and was recently named Retail Baker of the Year. Her sister owns a well-respected Pilates studio, and her other brother followed their father into the stock brokerage business.

Claudia's husband Pat is a governmental affairs director for the City of Everett. He is responsible for the political coordination of major projects in the community such as the construction of a US Naval base, and hopefully the addition of a branch campus of the University of Washington. Claudia is the daughter of a former city councilman, so local politics are near to her heart.

Her son is a college administrator by day, and a Seattle club DJ on weekends. Claudia's daughter is a master rower who competes in the US and internationally, coaches the crew team for her high school alma mater, and is completing her masters' degree at Seattle University. Claudia and her husband enjoy traveling for Tim's performances and Caitlin's rowing competitions.

In thirty-one years, the agency has moved and grown. Claudia has added new team members, including a childhood friend of her son, new products and new companies. Thanks to Quantum, she enjoys this business more today than she did 31 years ago. And since her father set an example for her of working as a broker until age 79, Claudia is hoping that she will be able to continue to grow her agency for many years to come!

Where did you first learn about Insurance Profit Systems, Inc. and the Quantum Club™?

After reading interesting, but hard-to-believe, full-page advertisements in the insurance trade press for a number of years, I finally signed up for a teleconference. I honestly don't remember which "Quantum Star" was the featured interviewee --- perhaps it was John Mason – but the pitch was compelling enough to have me run to the fax machine to quickly sign up, due to the limited number of openings, for membership.

What inspired you to try this program?

I have always been interested in finding new, and more efficient, ways to run my agency. I was an early member of George Nordhaus' Insurance Marketing and Management Systems. I was also very tired and discouraged. I was working too many hours, carrying too much of the customer service burden, and I didn't even know what the problem was. I wanted to deliver even better service for my clients. I wanted to provide additional opportunity for my employees. And I wanted to reclaim control over my life.

What are you doing differently in your business?

Everything! Although it took me a longer time than most Quantum agents to "get it" and start relinquishing some of the client-facing work, I now find that I am working "on" my business, and not "in" it.

My team members have stepped up and are producing new business, and servicing existing clients, more effectively than I had been, given the many hats I was wearing in a day. The quantity and quality of our client communication has improved dramatically. We are now "touching" our clients more than 15 times per year! We have developed systems for every process in our organization. We have discontinued our scatter-shot approach to marketing and have identified niches within our personal lines marketplace. This has allowed us to communicate with a much clearer and precise message, and it has provided a much improved ROI.

We have implemented Quantum principles to hire our gifted team. Over 50% of our team is new to the agency in the past year, and we have the strongest and most talented group of agents ever in our history.

What do you see as your "job"? What role do you play in your company?

My role has changed dramatically since joining IPS/QC. I am now the coach or GM, not the utility infielder. I am the conductor, not the base violinist. My role is to develop the systems, and the talent, so that my team can hit the home run or make the beautiful music come to life. After thirty plus years in the industry, I also take very seriously my responsibility to give back. I've made an effort to coordinate mastermind groups and seminars for younger or smaller agencies in my area. I gain a tremendous amount of personal satisfaction from cheering them on as they take massive steps toward future growth.

Talk to me about your specific marketing strategies.

Our major focus during this "soft market" has been "organic" growth --- growth that comes from within, or by referral from our existing base of clients and community contacts. This year, we developed our 5x5x5 Growth Strategy which will organically double our agency size in the next 5 years. The 3 legs of this strategy are:

5% Growth in New Clients --- through increased emphasis on our updated Referral Rewards Program and through community event sponsorships

5% Growth in the Number of Policies per Client --- through increased Cross Selling, Client Nurturing, and the addition of additional products and companies

5% Growth in the Average Premium Per Policy --- through renewal reviews that focus on increased protection for the client through higher liability limits, improved Insurance-to-Value on their home, increased jewelry schedules, etc.

Tell me about your experience with QC/IPS.

Last year, we also made the commitment to send team members to Quantum events so that they can experience first-hand QC energy and enthusiasm. Nick, our new business sales CSR, attended the Personal Lines Super Conference. Nathalie, our communications director, attended Boot Camp.

Laura, our customer service CSR, will attend one of the Closed Door Conferences in 2008.

In addition, all team members were enrolled in the CSR Mastery Program, and have benefited greatly from this program.

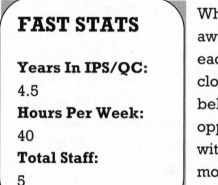

FAST STATS

Years In IPS/QC:
4.5
Hours Per Week:
40
Total Staff:
5

While there are many awesome features of each boot camp or closed door session, I believe that the opportunity to network with hundreds of the most marketing-savvy and growth-oriented agents in North America has had the greatest impact on how I am now approaching my business.

The reason that I say this is that while Michael Jans' training is absolutely first-class --- the very best in the industry --- the encouragement (and often prodding) to implement his ideas and principles has come from fellow Quantum members. It is my respected peer group that challenges me, by their example and their mentoring, to greater success than I could ever have imagined. Michael Jans should take full credit for this --- it is Michael that has created and nurtured this membership group.

Our business now has a clear roadmap for the future. Our team knows their role, and their professional rewards, if they support our goals. Our clients are better informed consumers and are more loyal. Our companies are thrilled to see agents in their distribution channel that are excited by growth and driven to success.

How has your personal life improved since joining IPS/QC?

I have more time for family. I am blessed to have a circle of friends and fellow Quantum members that support me. I no longer feel alone when faced with a difficult management situation. I have taken Quantum tools for planning and implemented them in my personal life to improve my health through more organized exercise regimens. I even have a Quantum mastermind group member who volunteered to hold me accountable to my health objectives!

What specific marketing advice or strategies would you give to another agent?

Borrow a Quantum idea, tweak it, personalize it, improve it, and make it your own. Then share it with others.

Don't get in your own way, don't over-think a marketing strategy, 80% is good enough – you can always modify it as you go.

Don't be reluctant to ask for advice. We've all learned from each other.

And most importantly, to quote the awesome Mike Stromsoe: "Execute, implement, and take action."

Why is this your Best Year Ever?

Last year was the year that Quantum strategies were implemented in an organized and systematic way. I helped form the Nexus mastermind group of 8 Quantum members who met monthly by teleconference, and in person at Quantum events. We helped each other to establish 30-60-90 day goals, and held each other accountable to those goals. Quantum tools, such as the Team Member Roadmap, Laser Focus Planner, 90 Day Planner,

Ultimate Agency Blueprint, Client Nurturing Calendar, and many others, were used daily.

Team members were invited to participate by attending Quantum events, enrolling in CSR Mastery Program, and joining Quantum-related mastermind groups. We focused on client nurturing through bi-monthly newsletters, ZIPDRIP, postcards, holiday cards and started measuring and benchmarking our organic growth. Our team was involved in setting and developing strategies for attaining our goals. The whole was far stronger than the many earlier parts! We also entered the Best Year Ever competition which kept us focused on our goals all year.

Claudia McClain's Secret Weapons

Claudia has worked hard to make her name recognizable in the area. She capitalizes on every opportunity to reach out to the community, decreases labor cost by employing interns, and tailors her mailings and give-aways to her demographic. Below we've detailed a few of the tactics she swears by.

The Agency Newsletter. A newsletter is a great way to reach out to current clients and get the attention of new ones. Keep the publication simple, easy to read, and include lots of photos, consumer tips, featured clients, and thank you messages.

The 80% Rule. Even if you don't have time to perfect and customize a mailing, get it out. Collect as many prospects as you can.

Customize Give-Aways. Find gifts that fit your niches and the season. Claudia has a lot of clients in education, so she gave away branded insulated lunch bags. During baseball season the agency handed out stadium blankets, and during daylight savings time- smoke detector batteries.

Take Advantage of Community Events. Claudia and her team sponsor a booth at her community's Night Out Against Crime event. A branded booth and a variety of branded give-aways offer amazing exposure for a low price.

Hire an Intern. Young people are willing to work for very little, if anything, to gain college credit and experience. Use a popular and inexpensive site like Craigslist to find an intern. The extra hands will lighten your clerical work load, and you just might be training a talented future team member.

2 - Joe Hershey

THE DIRTY DOZEN DIARIES

"I think it is human nature to resist change ... Going to sessions has truly helped me to stay motivated, to continually implement change, and kept me from falling back into old habits!"

-JOE HERSHEY

Joe Hershey's family has owned and managed insurance agencies since 1890. Insurance was the family business, a way of life, and the only natural career path for Joe. Immediately after he received a Bachelor of Science in Business Administration, he became a commercial lines underwriter in his father's company. He worked in that position for just over two years and then moved into a position as a marketing representative for the next two years. He had just started to manage a brokerage division when his father and his partners decided to sell the business.

Joe then began to learn about the financial services industry and began a career as a financial planner. He did not enjoy this, so after a year and a half he started to look for a retail agency that he could get involved with. His hope was to ultimately own and run the agency himself. After a short stint with the first agency, he joined the agency of his current business partner, Dennis Zubler. Today they share equal ownership.

Joe is married and has two daughters who are 10 and 14 years old. He and his family have centered their lives around God and value the time they spend together. Joe and his wife are generally very involved in their children's lives and in the community. They are board members, officers, and coaches on their children's sporting teams. Joe says his primary motivator in life is his family.

Where did you first learn about Insurance Profit Systems, Inc. and the Quantum Club™?

My business partner, Dennis Zubler, listened in on a teleconference done by IPS. He decided to join Quantum Club™. Immediately after joining, he said that I needed to be involved. He shared a few concepts with me – and I joined Quantum Club™ as a member the next month.

What inspired you to try this program?

My business partner's enthusiasm.

What are you doing differently in your business?

Everything is different! For example, I used to be the person who sat in the office, writing new commercial lines business, and servicing much of the business as well. Today, I don't answer the phone – or ever even take a phone call.

In the last year, I took 6 weeks of vacation. Prior to joining IPS I was lucky to get out of the office for more than 2 weeks – and when I came back, things weren't pretty. Today, when I return from vacation, I usually have some magazines and industry mail to look at. I am normally through my mail and e-mail by mid-morning of my first day back.

What do you see as your "job"? What role do you play in your company?

Today I spend 25% of my time in a managerial role and the rest of my time is spent on marketing and designing sales systems.

Talk to me about your specific marketing strategies.

I have always believed that niche marketing was the way to grow my business. However, every time I started to grow in a niche, the company would change something, or decide they didn't like the class, and my program would fall apart. This was my fault for having only one good carrier.

I did this a few different times prior to joining Quantum Club™. Today we are very successful with niche markets and I believe that this is for one reason: We've learned to market and run the business the IPS way. My previous attempts to niche market were flawed in many ways, and as a result, never worked. Michael has shown me how to re-design my agency and turn it into a true sales culture.

Tell me about your experience with QC/IPS.

I think that it is human nature to resist change. Human beings seem to be pulled by some gravitational force to do things the way they have always done them. For that reason, I have attended every boot camp held since I joined Quantum

Club™. I have also attended most of the closed-door training sessions and many other meetings.

Going to sessions has truly helped me to stay motivated, to continually implement change, and kept me from falling back into old habits!

Without a doubt, the one item I have learned that has had the greatest impact is the Rule of 46! The concept is that if you delegate 5% of your duties to your team, you will free up 46% of your time over the course of a year. The second part of this concept is that you must use this newly-freed up time to work on high-leverage tasks and duties. Michael Jans refers to this as working "on your business," not "in your business."

My agency is now growing at a much faster rate than ever before. When we were a very small insurance agency, it wasn't too difficult to have years where we grew 15 to 20%. However, as the agency continued to grow, the growth rate steadily declined, leaving me spending more time at work with fewer results. The agency had slowed to annual growth rates in the single digits during the hard market.

In the last few months, our gross revenue has been up 20 to 25% compared to the same period last year – and we are gaining momentum. Not only are the financial figures getting better, but also my team is more committed to the agency and running the day-to-day operation on their own.

How has your personal life improved since joining IPS/QC?

I have more time to spend with my family, doing the things that I enjoy now, than I have ever had since I began working full-time.

When I joined Quantum, I heard John Mason presenting. He told his story of how he was working 100-hour work weeks and was never home. A few years after joining Quantum Club™, his daughter asked him, "Why don't you work anymore?" You see, John had reduced his hours from 100 or more per week to less than 25. He was normally at home by the time his kids got off the school bus.

I recently experienced the same thing when my wife asked me why I wasn't working much anymore. To be fair and keep things in perspective, I must tell you that I have never worked 100 hours per week. However, I was working between 50 and 60 hours a week before I joined Quantum Club™. Now I work less than 40 hours per week, and some of that time is spent working from home (my wife assumes that if I'm at home, I'm not working – this explains why she thinks I never work). I make all of my kids' important events, school activities, and big games.

My personal life is good – and getting better every day.

What specific marketing advice or strategies would you give to another agent?

- Market more often.
- Be as specific as possible.
- Expand your marketing territory.
- Start thinking bigger!

Why is this your Best Year Ever?

My staff has been more motivated than ever! The team is working in harmony, taking care of the day-to-day operations of my business. When I come back after being out of the office for a week or two, the new business has continued to flow in and everything is running as it's supposed to. New business production is higher than it has ever been, and we put the systems and marketing in place to continue our substantial growth pattern for the next couple of years. All of these things came together in the last year, making this my Best Year Ever (YET)!

Joe Hershey's Secret Weapons

Joe has mastered one of the core principles of Quantum Club™: He has learned how to make his business work for him. Here are some of the strategies Joe relies on to streamline his office's workflow and boost efficiency.

Delegate. Joe and his partner do not take phone calls. A staff member handles all of the incoming calls, which frees up Joe to focus on planning and improving the agency.

Develop Procedures. Spend some time designing processes to make the office run more efficiently. Document all procedures and workflows so new employees can be quickly trained, and old employees have a quick reference tool.

Change the Culture. Changing the culture of the agency can inspire employees and promote growth. Rewards for good work serve as an employee incentive and progress can be tracked on a public board.

Business Client of the Month Spotlight

Since the spring of 1998, **Ironstone Rental** has been providing the local area with quality and well maintained rental equipment. They provide a wide range of items from lawn and garden equipment to larger construction equipment.

In addition to the rental business, they have a discount building materials business. This was started about 3 years ago and it has really taken off, providing the area with great pricing on a variety of items such as kitchen cabinets, flooring, composite decking, doors, and windows.

218 Hershey Road, Elizabethtown

Phone (717) 361-2626

www.ironstonerental.com

Client Appreciation Day

We appreciate all of our clients and we want to thank you for your business, your referrals, your testimonials, and your friendship.

Please be sure to join us on June 2 at 12:00 noon

for a pig roast, and a chance to win prizes of:

Jewelry

LCD TV

Laptop computer

Trip for 2

Cash

and more...

Please email Liz to let us know you are planning to be there. liz@homafiusinsurance.com

A Not-So-Trivial Pursuit

This month, Hornafius Insurance Agency is sponsoring a Trivia Contest and offering you a chance to win a valuable prize. Test your knowledge! Just one correct answer and you could be this month's winner. If more than one person has the exact answer, the winner will be the person whose entry reached our office first. Email your answer to liz@hornafiusinsurance.com, or write down your name and answer and then fax to 717-367-5827, or send your answer to 23 S Market St, Elizabethtown PA 17022. Good luck!

What explorer introduced pigs to North America?

Your Name _____   Your Answer _____

Hornafius Insurance Agency • (717) 367-5126 • info@hornafiusinsurance.com

3 – Dennis Zubler

Dennis started his career in the insurance industry in 1980 as an agent selling life insurance, health insurance, disability insurance, and mutual funds. After four and a half years, he took a position as the Business Manager at a general agency of Connecticut Mutual in their office in Harrisburg, Pennsylvania. Four years later he took a position as a Marketing Representative with Aetna in their property and casualty business. He later worked as a Marketing Representative for New Your Casualty Insurance Company and Harleysville Mutual Insurance Company. In April of 1994, Dennis went to Hornafius Insurance Agency with the understanding that he would purchase the agency in three years. Eighteen months later, on October 1, 1995, Dennis purchased the agency.

Dennis says he enjoys the business so much because he likes people. Working with and helping people are a primary motivator for Dennis. "A few years ago I did an exercise to help me determine what I truly wanted from life. The exercise starts by asking the question, "What's important about money to you?" At the end of the exercise you realize you have discovered what is MOST IMPORTANT to you. My final answer was: Achieving God's purpose for me." On his journey to find that answer, Dennis discovered other personal truths. He enjoyed helping mankind, knowing he made a difference, feeling like he had contributed, and experiencing a sense of accomplishment.

Dennis has a son, a daughter, and a granddaughter. His youngest child is a senior in college and has demonstrated that she can take care of herself. Dennis feels very fortunate that both of his children have done well in their young lives and seem to be in control of their future.

Because he derives so much pleasure from helping others, Dennis decided to set a lofty goal for himself: He would give a dollar for every dollar he spent. His target date to achieve this goal is January

2009. Dennis says the greatest satisfaction in his adult life comes from giving and helping others.

Where did you first learn about Insurance Profit Systems, Inc. and the Quantum Club™?

In January of 2004 I received a long letter in the mail - the kind that I usually just toss in the trash. However, something got me to read this particular letter. The letter told me about how I could have an insurance agency where everything was wonderful. Many things seemed too good to be true, but there was a teleconference that promised to explain everything.

What inspired you to try this program?

A few days later, I was listening to the teleconference and learning about the many great things that I could get from my business. Again, some things sounded too good to be true, but because there was a money back guarantee and a limited time offer, I called immediately after the teleconference and joined IPS and QC. This was one of the best business decisions I have ever made.

What are you doing differently in your business?

Over the past 3 and a half years the business has gone through a dramatic transformation. Today, I own a business that works for me, instead of me working for the business. I have a business where the employees (referred to as the TEAM) handle the day-to-day activities of the business. I have a TEAM that has goals to make the business money and be successful.

Prior to IPS & QC I was busy handling day-to-day activities and did not have time to lead the business into the future.

What do you see as your "job"? What role do you play in your company?

Today my job is to create a vision for where I want the business to go in the next year, five years, and ten years. Joe and I are currently in the process of purchasing another insurance agency about 60 miles away. We can do this because we have a TEAM handling the day-to-day activities in our current business. When we purchase that agency we will need to spend a lot of time bringing that business operation up to speed with our current business. We will be able to do that because of our TEAM.

Because of IPS & QC, we have a business that is much more efficient and profitable than before. Today Joe and I have time to plan, strategize, and focus on the future instead of being bogged down in the daily activities of the business.

Talk to me about your specific marketing strategies.

Because this industry is constantly changing, I believe both diversity and focus are important. I believe that a large number of small to medium size clients provides more stability than a smaller number of large clients. Therefore, I want to maintain a profitable volume of personal lines business along with a profitable volume of commercial lines business. We encourage referrals from both clients and non-clients. We also have started and developed profitable niche marketing programs. Last year, the niche marketing programs have accounted for a little over 50% of our new business.

Tell me about your experience with QC/IPS.

Both Joe and I attend almost every training session provided by IPS. Every event has turned into a good investment. When I first joined IPS & QC I was in awe of some of the members and a little intimidated. However, I tried to learn as much as I could from Michael Jans and several other QC members and emulate what they were doing.

FAST STATS

Years In IPS/QC:
3.5
Hours Per Week:
35
Total Staff:
6

The reason that I made the top twelve this past year was because of my desire to be like many of those members that have been honored before. I would say that I can't afford to miss the IPS training events.

There were two experiences that had a tremendous impact on me. The first was the John Mason story - and meeting John and hearing the story from him. The second was watching the top ten at the 2006 Boot Camp and saying to myself, "How can I be up there on stage next year?" At the 2006 Boot Camp I knew that Joe and I were positioned to have a good year. We had a good TEAM in place. On the plane back to Harrisburg, I decided I was going to do everything I could to make the top ten last year. During that flight I came up with the idea of having a Best Year Ever contest for our TEAM. That contest was very successful and created a great deal of self motivation among the TEAM. They also continued throughout the year to develop and improve as a TEAM.

Today I have a business that works for me. Our business operation is much more efficient. Everyone in the business understands his or her role and responsibilities. Everyone is working to make the business successful. Because of this we are having greater growth than ever before. Joe and I now have time to focus on the future direction of the business and expect this year to be a better year than last year.

How has your personal life improved since joining IPS/QC?

I have more money and more time for my personal life than ever before. I take more vacations because I have the time and money to do it. One of my goals is to take a week of vacation every month. I hope I can achieve that within the next two years.

In May of next year I plan to spend the entire month in Brazil. As I mentioned earlier, I have a personal goal to give a dollar for every dollar I spend on consumption, and hope to achieve this goal by January 2009. This is certainly a dramatic improvement to my personal life.

What specific marketing advice or strategies would you give to another agent?

Use the IPS tools for marketing. DO NOT take short cuts. Do the work and then implement, tweak, implement, tweak and you will be successful. Be a good student and learn from Michael Jans. Read EVERYTHING Michael puts out and discover how you can use his techniques and strategies. Michael's copywriting hooked me and I'm thankful for that.

Why is this your Best Year Ever?

I have more control, more money, and more time off. I expect all of these will continue to increase as we move forward. We have a great TEAM working in the business. I have spent less time "working in the business" and more time "working on the business." The business continues to operate successfully even when I am not there.

Dennis Zubler's Secret Weapons

Dennis's philosophy is that you must have an effective team plan if you want to be successful. Hire carefully, and train your team well. Here's how Dennis makes it happen.

Know What You Want. Knowing what you want requires setting goals. Dreams are important, but writing down those dreams in the form of attainable goals is the only way to make your dreams a reality. Dennis highly recommends <u>Goals</u> by Brian Tracy.

Hire the Right People. Dennis and his partner hire employees based on attitude and ability to learn. He recommends profiling every potential member of your team, and always ask, "In your previous job, how did you contribute to the company?" An answer to that question is mandatory if an applicant is to be considered.

Assign Positions. Profile current employees to determine their strengths, and assign them roles that suit them well. Be the leader. Make sure all members of the team understand their roles.

Listen to Your Team. Dennis and his partner allow his team to design binders to help monitor their progress. Besides following agency-established tools and guidelines, employees are encouraged to develop their own tools. The creativity of your staff is an often untapped source. Use your staff to brainstorm new methods.

THE HONEST FEEDBACK EVALUATION FORM

How are we doing?

Your comments are the most valuable information we have to help us improve our service to you. *Please* take a few minutes of your time to let us know what you found most valuable and what you expect of us.

You don't have to respond, *but we really hope you do!*

Brutal honesty is greatly appreciated!

What have we done well to serve you?
May we share your comments with others?   Yes ☐ No ☐
What did you like or value the most about buying insurance from Hornafius Insurance ?

What, if anything, would you like us to change or improve?
May I share these comments with our insurance companies and their underwriters? Yes ☐ No ☐
Is there any coverage or service or other special topic in insurance that you would like us to focus on during the coming year or through some other service?
My email address is: _____

Your Name _____

Please return to: We love referrals!

23 South Market Street, Elizabethtown, PA 17022; fax 717-367-5827
Email: dennis@hornafiusinsurance.com

69

4 – Bill Holland

THE DIRTY DOZEN DIARIES

"Because we have goals and systems in place to achieve these goals, my businesses have more reason to exist."

-BILL HOLLAND

Bill Holland started out working in radio broadcasting during college. He wrote copy, produced, and sold local commercials. He also produced an early morning radio program which featured news, disk jockey work, and interviews. He kept that job for the first ten years of his life after college. Bill says that working in radio broadcasting and advertising was a tremendous experience to have as a young man, but he really wanted to be an entrepreneur. He just did not quite understand how to make it work.

After a stint in the U.S. Air Force during the Vietnam conflict, Bill returned home and desperately needed a job. His brother-in-law was a successful insurance agent who thought Bill would do well in the business. Bill, however, was not excited about insurance. Insurance sales seemed much too boring. However, he needed to work, and his cousin told him about an opening for a State Farm agent in Savannah, Georgia. That was 1972, and Bill needed a job badly, so he decided to give the industry a shot.

Still reluctant about the insurance business, Bill moved to Savannah and opened a new agency. Having only two weeks of insurance training, he was truly starting from scratch. Thirty six years later, Bill is still working in Savannah as a State Farm agent.

Bill now admits that insurance was an excellent career choice. Many doors of opportunity have been opened, allowing Bill to get involved in other entrepreneurial endeavors like real estate investment. Investing, which has contributed substantially to his retirement funding, has also been very rewarding and exciting for Bill.

Bill is very happy with his life outside the business as well. Because most of his time during the week is spent working *on* his business—and not so much *in* the business, Bill has more time to do the things he loves. A favorite pastime is boating, and Bill spends hours just riding and enjoying the creeks and rivers near his home in coastal Georgia.

Bill developed an interest in his heath after being diagnosed as a type two diabetic early in 2006. Prior to this event he did not take physical fitness very seriously. Now he enjoys taking care of his health and keeping in shape. He has a full-time fitness trainer who helps him stay fit. Bill says, "After all, my body is the only one I have, and I really like living." And Bill has a lot of living to do. Thanks to the freedom afforded him by his success as an agent; Bill has the time and financial means to truly enjoy life.

Where did you first learn about Insurance Profit Systems, Inc. and the Quantum Club™?

Like many other insurance professionals in North America and beyond, I was on one of Michael's mailing lists. I kept getting these crazy looking flyers about how I could make tons of money, build amazing growth, and have lots of vacation time if I subscribed to one of his e-mails. So, I jumped on board and have been "hooked" ever since. I later joined Quantum Club™ and attended my first Boot Camp in 2003.

My life and business have been improving ever since. Every day I learn something new I can use to help attain my goals, be a better business manager, and develop my dreams as an entrepreneur.

What inspired you to try this program?

I was inspired by Michael's presentation at my first Boot Camp in Chicago. My excitement was heightened by the enthusiasm of other Quantum Club™ members. They all seemed so pumped up and willing to unselfishly share their successes and techniques. This really impressed me, and I quickly got attached to the club. I appreciated Michael's tireless efforts to keep us on track and in tune with what it takes to develop and execute your dreams for your business, and his encouragement to keep stretching for the next level of achievement.

What are you doing differently in your business?

I am spending more time each day working *on* the business instead of just *in* it. This has really turned things around for me. Even though I am almost 65, which seems to be the normal age to stop working, I no longer think of retirement. I am just getting started. I have a new zeal for life and for creating new and exciting techniques to make my businesses work more efficiently and profitably.

My zest for growth has shot through the roof. Using the strategies and techniques I have learned in Quantum Club™, my business is on track to grow 20 % / year.

What do you see as your "job"? What role do you play in your company?

My job is to inspire my companies to grow profitably and create opportunities for each of my team members. I provide leadership. I am the spark plug that ignites imagination from each team member. I can only continue to succeed if the team succeeds. They depend on my ideas and enthusiasm to guide them through these endeavors. I love watching them grow and mature in the business. All these exciting developments have come about since joining Quantum Club™.

Talk to me about your specific marketing strategies.

Marketing is in the DNA of my business. My specific marketing strategies begin with adding value to my product. True insurance involves much more than simply delivering satisfactory service. My strategy is to take the person from a prospect, to a customer, to a client, and ultimately, to a raving fan. This is the challenge I put before my team members every day in our meetings.

We want to develop as many raving fans as possible. Every raving fan is a cheerleader for our business. They work for us, sending business to us with their recommendation. With their help, the sale is made even before we meet the referred client. The referrals are already interested in buying; now we just have to help identify their needs and offer appropriate products, our objective being to convert them into raving fans.
This is very rewarding. Part of our daily operations includes reviewing the testimonials of our customers. Reading what raving fans have written about their feelings towards our business is exciting and rewarding for us.

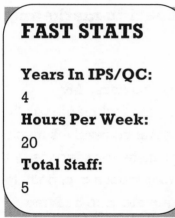

FAST STATS

Years In IPS/QC:
4
Hours Per Week:
20
Total Staff:
5

Tell me about your experience with QC/IPS.

I have attended every boot camp since 2003, including one Advanced Boot Camp. I have also attended most of the Closed Door Sessions since 2004. I am now participating in the first Agency Mastery Program, and my team is involved in Michael's year long CSR Mastery Program. I also participate in Quantum PLUS. I am learning to work more *on* my businesses instead of *in* them.

My company has transformed into a much more professional business that strives to deliver a value-added product to the customer. This transformation is now much more evident in my office, because each team member is also influenced by the IPS principles that have been introduced. Because we have goals and systems in place to achieve these goals, my businesses have more reason to exist.

How has your personal life improved since joining IPS/QC?

My personal life is now more organized and enjoyable. Whether I am attending to business or enjoying life with family and friends, my days are filled with purpose. I am able to see real progress in my personal life thanks to the systems I learned in Quantum Club™. I use many of these principles to enjoy life.

What specific marketing advice or strategies would you give to another agent?

I would suggest the agent learn to work more *on* their business and stop trying to do everything at the office on his or her own.

Why is this your Best Year Ever?

This is my best year every because I was able to move up to the Next Level. After being selected to be a part of the Dirty Dozen, and being recognized by my peers at Boot Camp in Chicago this year, I saw a new me. I was able to see the progress I had made both in my business and in my personal life.

I could never find the words to express the sense of accomplishment I feel. One simply has to personally experience this kind of success to understand. Reaching the peak is truly great when you have struggled in the climb.

Bill Holland's Secret Weapons

Bill believes in making a strong impression - both on his clients and on his team. Here are three ways Bill makes his mark and demonstrates his appreciation.

Harness The Power of Testimonials. Bill highly recommends using testimonials as part of your marketing strategy. Simply ask customers, "What do you like about working with this agency?" The answers become powerful, real endorsements you can use in every aspect of your marketing campaign.

"Wow" Your Prospects. Use the first twenty days after speaking with a prospect to demonstrate the benefits of working with your agency. Prepare a welcome kit full of small gifts, send personal thank you letters, and ask for testimonials.

Appreciate Team Members. Pay them well and recognize their talents. Give bonuses based on production. When a staff member does well, offer a small reward. Bill says even something small, like taking an employee to lunch and getting to know him or her personally, can really build loyalty to the company. Employees will work harder for an agent if they feel appreciated and respected.

Tell Others About Us And Get a $10 Gas Card!

Referrals are the lifeblood of any business, and there's no better source than you, our clients. This month, we honor:

For spreading the word about our agency and bringing us new clients we will present YOU with a **$10.00 Gas Card.**

Next month's referral business prize winner could be you. Just mention Bill Holland Insurance Agency to a friend, relative, customer, colleague, whomever. Thank you in advance.

"Every day, you'll have opportunities to take chances and to work outside your safety net. Sure, it's a lot easier to stay in your comfort zone... in my case, business suits and real estate... but sometimes you have to take risks. When the risks pay off, that's when you reap the biggest rewards."

Donald Trump

```
Bill Holland Insurance Agency
11712 Largo Drive
Savannah Georgia 31419
912-927-2288
```

5 – Shaun Irwin

Shaun Irwin started at the Anderson Agency answering the phone and opening the mail. He had just moved to the area from San Diego, and needed a job. He talked his way in and learned from square one. That was in 1987.

Eleven years later he bought the company from the family that had started the agency in 1927. Now being the owner of his own agency, family, and the idea of being part of a broader community are what drives Shaun. He is a learner- a self proclaimed voracious reader- who values education. He wants his children to be learners and enjoys being able to provide a quality education for his children.

Shaun's success also allows him to give back a little, as well as spend time with his family. He enjoys the many opportunities for charitable involvement his industry affords, and he loves to travel with his family and show his children various parts of the country and the world.

Where did you first learn about Insurance Profit Systems, Inc. and the Quantum Club™?

In a magazine advertisement.

What inspired you to try this program?

I spent years learning the technical aspects of the insurance business. I thought it was time to learn about marketing.

What are you doing differently in your business?

I am thinking in terms of abundance instead of scarcity, managing my time better, allowing the people I work with to grow instead of doing everything myself, and marketing more effectively and more often. I am also investing in other businesses so that the income generated from this business is multiplied in another endeavor.

What do you see as your "job"? What role do you play in your company?

I am the CEO, planner, strategist, marketer, team motivator, and innovator.

Talk to me about your specific marketing strategies.

I utilize direct mail, ZIPDRIP, newsletters, telemarketing, seminars, fax, Web sites, Automated Response Technologies (ART), hotlines and referral rewards.

Tell me about your experience with QC/IPS.

I attend at least four events per year.

For me, the best part of boot camps is being surrounded by other professionals working on their businesses and getting ideas and the positive energy to continue the journey.

I now have more money, more control, and more time off!!! I play 75 rounds of golf in the summer and take eight to ten weeks of vacation each year.

How has your personal life improved since joining IPS/QC?

My personal life has been the most radical change for me since joining IPS. This could not have come at a better time in my life. I had and still have young children so freeing up time to be with them and being there for them is the single biggest benefit of IPS/Quantum for me. My wife and I are involved in coaching their sports, volunteering at school, and helping them grow and blossom - probably too much for their liking sometimes!

What specific marketing advice or strategies would you give to another agent?

Do something, anything to get the ball rolling and then keep doing it. The old baseball saying of "Hit it till your hands bleed," is true with marketing.

Why is this your Best Year Ever?

I have the complete confidence that we are on the right track in our personal and business lives!

Shaun Irwin's Secret Weapons

Shaun says his plan of attack is simple and effective: Be direct. By being assertive and proactive, Shaun has built a successful business and a team of satisfied and motivated employees.

Just Do It. Shaun's number one strategy is to just go for it. Be assertive, ask for the sale, and proudly advertise your agency's expertise. Encourage your team to be direct with every client.

Give Your Agents A Voice. Fundraising for charity is a part of most agency referral programs. Shaun allows his team members to choose the charities, which serves as a great motivator and helps build loyalty.

Micro-niches. As an agent, you can be an expert in any particular niche. How do you become an expert? Invest in niches and micro-niches, offer individual services, and advertise your expertise.

YOUR Friends And Our 2,019 Satisfied Clients Say It Best...

"I can always depend on them!"
"It's very simple, the Anderson agency are friendly people that provide great service. It's nice to know that when it comes to my Insurance needs, I can always depend on them."

Scott Thorp

"They have saved me money!"
"They have saved me money—over 30% reduction in premium. I had a couple of claims and they dealt with it immediately and everything went quickly and no hassles."

ACS Holdings, Inc

"Thank you for your dedicated service!"
"We've known Shaun Irwin since 1986. He's a great friend and an excellent insurance broker. Thanks for your dedicated service!"

Keith & Abby Mackey

"We saved $3,183!"
"We saved $3,183 when we switched our insurance to them. They are always there for us to answer questions and help with claims."

Margarita Wilson, Armor Security

"WOW!! Great!"
"I've been with the agency, Wight and now Anderson since 1956 - WOW!!! Great."

Roger Waller

THE DIRTY DOZEN DIARIES

"I talk their language, hit their hot buttons, and listen to their problems."

-TOM LARSEN

For twelve and a half years Tom worked at the agency of a friend, who eventually got him interested in the insurance business. He has now been in business for four and a half years.

Tom does his best to keep in shape by working out often, which must be working. He's still playing baseball and fast-pitch softball at 50, and likes to play golf and travel.

Tom believes that to be successful you need to hang around people with new ideas and new ways to market. You have to learn from the changes they have made in their business models. He has followed his own advice, learning from other

Quantum Club™ agents, and studying the systems that work. The secret to Tom's success is in his detailed marketing plan. He emphasizes customer appreciation, and believes in boldly following your instincts, even if your plans fall outside of traditionally accepted marketing techniques.

Where did you first learn about Insurance Profit Systems, Inc. and the Quantum Club™?

I think I saw a magazine advertisement in 1998 or 1999.

FAST STATS

Years In IPS/QC:
3.5
Hours Per Week:
35
Total Staff:
6

What inspired you to try this program?

I was experiencing stagnant sales, and I felt like my agency was not standing out from any other agency out there.

What are you doing differently in your business?

We are treating the client differently. We are ranking them, up selling them, and keeping in constant communication with them. I am trying to be a trusted advisor and not an insurance salesman.

What do you see as your "job"? What role do you play in your company?

I am the marketer for Larsen & Associates. My job is to get the phone to ring, and to set in motion the sales cycle. I market, and my staff writes business for me.

Talk to me about your specific marketing strategies.

I am a former restaurant owner, so I use that to my advantage to market to restaurants. I talk their language, hit their hot buttons, and listen to their problems. I am also a landlord, so I market to that segment too. I speak at their functions, send out newsletters, and attend meetings.

Tell me about your experience with QC/IPS.

I particularly enjoy round table discussions at Boot Camp, where agency owners from around the country share their best ideas. I also benefit from the discussions out in the hall, at lunch, over a drink – you learn a lot about others' businesses and changes they have made themselves.

I now own my own agency. When I first joined I was a producer at another agency.

How has your personal life improved since joining IPS/QC?

I was able to upgrade to a nicer home in one of the best communities of Buffalo. I drive newer cars every three years, and my daughter is at Boston College this year.

What specific marketing advice or strategies would you give to another agent?

Make all of your INTERNAL changes first, before you get to the external marketing. We all know the external marketing is "sexy and new," but have you maxed out your current relationships? Cross selling and up selling internally should be your first priority.

Why is this your Best Year Ever?

We have increased our revenue, and increased the bottom line. This is my second year with my Mastermind group, and we have identified more niches that we may pursue.

Tom Larsen's Secret Weapons

Tom uses a variety of tactics to grow his business. He believes in categorizing clients, appreciating their business, and giving back. He also highly recommends getting expert advice and support from a mentor. Here are a few details of Tom's multi-faceted plan.

Segmentation. Segmenting their business books allows agents to track the source of their profits. All customers should be appreciated, but a tiered system establishes a frame of reference.

Treat Top Clients Well. Tom spends a little more to demonstrate his appreciation for top clients. For example, he offers a defensive driving course and a 10% discount to platinum level customers. Those clients share the benefits with friends, which naturally increases the number of prospects.

Get a Mentor. Find someone you can lean on, and who motivates you. Having an experienced professional available for questions, that you can call regularly and will help you take your business to the next level.

Inject Personality Into Your Marketing. Clients like to work with personable, relatable agents. Be yourself. For example, Tom sent a sales letter to veterinarians that had been "written" by his dog. The creative and funny mailer got a lot more attention than a traditional sales pitch.

Include Charity. For every referral, Tom gives $5 to a charity. He creates a report card about the agency's contributions to help pump up the referral program. Tom recommends doing quarterly referral programs, and getting the charities involved.

92

7 – Ed Cantu

Ed graduated with a Bachelor of Business Administration degree in Personnel Management from Texas A&M Corpus Christi in 1981. His first job after graduation was with a car rental company that specialized in providing vehicles for people who were involved in car accidents.

Ed worked hard for the company, becoming a district manager by age 23. But within two years, Ed had become frustrated. He was tired of working for managers who did not know how to treat employees. Ed believed there must be a better way to run a business efficiently and still treat workers fairly and with respect, so he decided to try something else. Determined to find success on his own, Ed answered an insurance company's classified ad. He has owned his agency for 22 years.

One of the best advantages of his approach to business, says Ed, is the amount of time he has available to spend with his lovely wife. Ed married his college sweetheart in 1993. Together they enjoy spending time and traveling with family and friends.

Ed also uses his newfound free time to enjoy his favorite activities - golf, and attending college and professional sporting events. (He serves on two Boards within the Athletic Department at Texas A&M - Corpus Christi.) Ed is able to combine business with pleasure, as he actively participates in the Home Builders Association of Corpus Christi Area and the Corpus Christi Board of Realtors.

Ed is a semi-captive agent of Farmers Insurance, which means that he is allowed to have other contracts and work with other companies. Of the 1,400 Farmers agents in Texas, Ed had spent several years in the top ten, but the Texas mold problems of 2000 threw his agency into a downward tail spin.

Like so many of the agents who gravitate towards IPS and QC, Ed faced a serious decline in business, and knew he needed to do something drastic to get his company back on track. Ed was in desperate search of a better plan. He realized the best way to recover would be to change direction and reinvent his agency. Ed became proactive, gathering information from QC and other agents that he could use to stop the bleeding, and start growing.

Where did you first learn about Insurance Profit Systems, Inc. and the Quantum Club™?

I was on IPS's mailing/fax broadcast list and I took part in one of their free tele-seminars after the second or third time they contacted me in 2001.

What are you doing differently in your business?

I use High Impact Marketing that attracts, converts, and retains clients, and I make sure my staff understands that we provide protection and not a commodity. We sell the value of our service, which includes our recommendations, to avoid unnecessary risk. We do not sell on price even when we have the best price available.

What do you see as your "job"? What role do you play in your company?

My role is to attract new clients and set up systems to make sure all operations run on auto pilot so that the agency grows and improves whether I'm at the office or not. I'm no longer a technician. I rarely sell or meet with clients. I work *on* my business not *in* my business.

Talk to me about your specific marketing strategies.

I run marketing campaigns that are geared toward my preferred niches: Homeowners, Restaurant Owners, and Apartment Complex Owners. I utilize multi-media including a referral program, direct mail, and print advertising that send the same message. I also use free hotlines and my Web site (www.edcantuinsurance.com) to add credibility.

Another key thing I recommend is to find an association that you want to deal with, such as a homebuilder's association, get involved with that association, and hope that the members will recognize you as being an expert and send referrals to you.

Tell me about your experience with QC/IPS.

I have attended every boot camp since 2001 and attend 1 to 3 workshops each year.

> "I have learned how to turn prospects into customers, customers into clients, clients into advocates and advocates into raving fans by better cross selling and nurturing clients."

The tools and concepts that Quantum Club™ teaches are wonderful. But the best part of the workshops is networking and exchanging ideas with successful agency principals from all over the U.S. and Canada.

My agency has grown each of the 7 years I have been a member of Quantum Club™. Last year saw the greatest growth with 27%. I have learned how to turn prospects into customers, customers into clients, clients into advocates and advocates into raving fans by better cross selling and nurturing clients.

> "Don't sell the carrier or carriers you may represent, sell your Unique Selling Proposition."

How has your personal life improved?

I have learned how to build a gifted staff of hard working team members who look for ways to improve themselves and our operations.

What specific marketing advice or strategies would you give to another agent?

Your marketing strategy must tell your reader, viewer, or listener why they should do business with only you. Don't sell the carrier or carriers you may represent, sell your Unique Selling Proposition.

Why is this your Best Year Ever?

We saw the most policy growth in several years (27%), increased commission (21%), loss ratios were less than 21%, improved my policies per household count to 2.8, and I replaced and/or added gifted team members who now place the goals of the agency over their own goals.

> He refuses to sell mono-line policies, unless there is a possibility for additional coverage.

Ed Cantu's Secret Weapons

Ed and his team make a point of setting their agency apart from all the others. They are able to accomplish this by offering clients a level of quality and value that other agencies simply cannot match. Ed does not try to sell cheap insurance or minimum liability protection. There are no quick fixes, pre-packaged deals for Ed's clients. He tells every potential customer, "We're professionals-we'll make suggestions based on your individual situation." Ed and his team gather enough information from each client to offer a proposal for car insurance, home insurance, life insurance and umbrellas. He refuses to sell mono-line policies, unless there is a possibility for additional coverage. Some clients are reluctant to offer so much information upfront, but Ed gently encourages them by explaining, "We want to protect your whole household. We can't do that if you have your life coverage somewhere else, because you might have some coverage gaps we don't know about."

Cross Sell and Up Sell Whenever Possible. Sell three or four policies to one person as opposed to selling one policy to three or four. And encourage your staff to expect customers to buy multiple policies. That expectation will lead to sales.

Distribute a Monthly Newsletter. Ed and his team send out about six-hundred copies to VIP clients, and about five or six hundred to realtors, mortgage companies, and other people who may send referrals. The newsletter is not a hard sell. Instead, Ed includes seasonal and current information that readers may find useful. For example, an issue may feature tips to protect your home from break-ins or ways to improve your car's fuel economy. Ed also spotlights a client on the back of each issue to say thank you. Clients who own a business really appreciate the free advertising.

Initiate a Referral Program. For example, every time somebody sends a referral, reward him or her with a small gift of appreciation, like a gift certificate for lunch at a local restaurant. Drawings for monthly prizes and an extravagant annual grand prize are also an excellent incentive. (Ed never forgets to announce the winners in the newsletter.) Additionally, Ed has had tremendous success raising money for March of Dimes by making a contribution for every referral received.

Motivate Your Team. Create immediate and long-term incentives for your employees. Ed offered cash rewards to employees for every customer they asked about life insurance. Once they reached the quota, Ed even presented them with a percentage of his contingency check.

Focus on Retention. The key is offering to provide protection, even if the client turns down the proposal. In the future, your offer will come to mind. Ed's office uses a grid to record the names of people who have been offered life insurance. Follow-ups, such as a call reminding a client of an age-based rate increase the week before the client's thirty-fifth birthday, are all scheduled and recorded in the grid.

Take Advantage of Location and Events. Ed saw great success with a cross-sale flood insurance program. Flood insurance is not required in Texas, but Ed's team was able to sell 130 policies to coastal area residents. Agents started calling around the beginning of hurricane season and followed up with clients the day after the area received eleven inches of rain.

8 – Terry Young

THE DIRTY DOZEN DIARIES

"QC has totally transformed my agency's operation. We are not the same company we were 3 years ago."

-TERRY YOUNG

Terry Young's very first job was in construction. Then he worked for Metropolitan Insurance Company selling life insurance. He spent 5 years in outside sales and marketing for a postage meter company, and eventually became a manager. His last year and a half with that company he was a sales trainer at the national training center. Most of his working life, about 25 years, Terry has spent in the independent agency system.

Insurance is Terry's career, real estate is his passion, and his hobby is NASCAR. But Terry recently developed a passion for something new - public speaking. He's had many opportunities to speak to groups of every size, but always as a course of business. Until this year, he never thought of speaking for training, education, or even entertainment purposes. Now, Terry has discovered he really enjoys speaking to groups, and takes every opportunity to do so.

Real estate motivates Terry, because he enjoys the business, but his real inspiration comes from his family. Terry has been married for 19 years, and has two beautiful daughters, one 15 and one 12.

Terry so deeply appreciates his family, he says, because of the experiences he had growing up. His parents divorced when he was 13, and his father died when Terry was 17. From that point, Terry was totally on his own. Because he didn't really have time with his parents, Terry vowed to give his family what he thinks is the most precious thing in the world: time. "My kids and wife get time with me, and there is nothing more valuable," says Terry.

Money is a satisfier for Terry, but not a motivator. Terry believes that while money takes care of his wants and needs, family and goals are what really drive him to succeed. He spends a lot of time working on his personal business journal, which he keeps with him at all times. The journal includes his set goals for the year, and a detailed plan about his purpose, reason, persistence, and the expected income from that goal.

Terry is tremendously successful today, but his story did not start out as well as he would have liked. After a 19 year old Terry racked up an impressively long list of driving offenses, a tough municipal court judge uttered a phrase that Terry now uses as a powerful marketing strategy. Money loves speed. The judge had intended to teach Terry a lesson about responsibility. He had no idea that, years later, Terry would turn that lesson into a hugely profitable business.

Where did you first learn about Insurance Profit Systems, Inc. and the Quantum Club™?

In the summer of 2004, my CFO was getting mailings and CD's from Michael Jans.

What inspired you to try this program?

At first I had nothing to do with it, but my CFO said, "Terry, do something with this or I'm canceling the membership and dropping the whole thing." So, in January of 2005 I went away for two days and brought Boot Camp in a Box with me. I read everything and watched every video in that box.

By the time I came back, I had been bitten by the QC and high impact marketing bug. I have been an avid reader, student, and implementer of QC principles since.

What are you doing differently in your business?

The number one thing I do differently is that I have a totally new mindset. I work *on* my business not *in* my business. I do something Michael shared in boot camp, called LEGS, which stands for Lead And Execute Growth Strategies. I've actually been using that strategy since learning it in QC.

The other big thing I learned was that I don't need outside sales people knocking on doors to make my business function. Now I use a system of tools, campaigning and copy to find motivated buyers. There are people in pain and need, and we are able to market to them using mass mail, mass email, mass video and mass voice broadcast.

What do you see as your "job"? What role do you play in your company?

Prior to QC, I considered myself a technician and manager. Now I am a manager entrepreneur.

Talk to me about your specific marketing strategies.

My agency is a niche marketer. We always have been, but never to this level. I'm able to use QC tools to drill down the niche into sub-niches and hyper-niches including different classes of business. We only use inside sales, and we always have multiple campaigns running at any given time. If one fails, the whole program doesn't fail.

Tell me about your experience with QC/IPS.

I have only missed one event in 3 years. I go to boot camp and all closed quarterly sessions and workshops. I also attend new member orientation every year, even though I've been a member for 3 years. That's where you gain knowledge and information. Networking with peers from all over the country is the key to my success. The opportunity to mix and mingle with other professionals is extremely powerful. I also learn so much from breakout sessions, where other agencies share what they are doing that's taken their organization up a notch.

I have more revenue, more clients, more time off, more employees, a bigger organization, more profit, higher retention, and more freedom and control. QC has totally transformed my agency's operation. We are not the same company we were 3 years ago.

How has your personal life improved since joining IPS/QC?

My personal life has never been better. I have more time with my kids and my wife. I have more money to provide the things I want to provide for them. I'm on the top of the world. I've learned how to nurture family, and they nurture me back. We write letters. I actually hand write letters to them in my journal. And when I go out of town, I hide cards for them in the house, and I mail those cards and letters, too. My 15 year old gave me a very powerful, hand written letter that was full of her thoughts, comments, and insights about what's going on in her life. It's one thing to talk with your family, but actually writing letters to each other on paper takes more thought. I have the time for that now.

What specific marketing advice or strategies would you give to another agent?

Create systems to get the phone to ring instead of trying to go out and hunt people that want to buy. Find the motivated buyers through various campaigns and tools within the organization.

When sending out mailings, we got attention by using "lumpy" envelopes. For example, we used multiple pieces. We never sent the same color envelope or the same color paper. One of the things that we did, and we used this also in the cabinet shop program, is hire a cabinet shop to cut us some 4x4 square pieces of wood, which we wrote on, stamped, and mailed.

Also, we figured out after a few months that when we mailed a piece out on Monday, we got more calls.

Why this is your Best Year Ever?

We experienced an agency growth of 40%. My personal income increased 200%. Overall, it's been an awesome, awesome year.

Terry Young's Secret Weapons

Terry has used his colorful life experience to build a dynamite marketing system. These tactics are all about going after what you want.

Money Loves Speed. Never lose track of the main goal: To get the marketing piece out the door. Don't spend too much time revising and searching for perfection-get the pieces out so they can start generating revenue.

Understand the 5 Business Components. People, Capital, Market, Product, and Organization are the five elements of every successful business. Learning to juggle and incorporate these elements into every aspect of your marketing plan is the best way to become an effective and profitable business.

Active Recruiting. Don't wait until you have an open position in your agency to start recruiting. Terry and his team use a ZIPDRIP email recruitment system that regularly advertises a need for a specific type of person. Dozens of people get the mailing and/or listen to a hotline message about the company. Now when Terry needs an employee, he has a large pool of interested applicants waiting to be screened.

Agency Acquisition. Starting from a list of thousands, Terry narrowed his options down to small town agencies. After sending out three acquisition letters and creating a nondisclosure agreement, Terry was able to merge with an agent in North Carolina, which resulted in tremendous profit.

9 – Jimmy McElreath

If experience has anything to do with success, Jimmy McElreath is a prime example. After graduating from college Jimmy worked as an Agriculture Extension Agent, was an agency manager with North Carolina Farm Bureau for eight years, and started his own agency in 1980. As a thirty year veteran in the industry, Jimmy has picked up more tricks and developed more effective marketing strategies than the average agent.

The best part of success as an agent, says Jimmy, is that he spends more time with his family and away from work.

Where did you first learn about Insurance Profit Systems, Inc. and the Quantum Club™?

I responded to an advertisement in the Best Review magazine and called the phone number. I then started to get mailings from Michael. I joined in August of 2006.

What inspired you to try this program?

I was inspired by the comments in Michael's mailings from other agents about the program. How did we get the rest of the staff on board? When the staff started to fall off a bit, we wanted to bring something new into the program to get them back on board.

We made some mistakes and we learned, but the staff came on board when they saw other people doing well.

What do you see as your "job"? What role do you play in your company?

I am the President and CEO. I handle the overall management. The change I made was to hire an operations manager. I delegate much more now.

FAST STATS

Years In IPS/QC:
1
Hours Per Week:
32
Total Staff:
11

Talk to me about your specific marketing strategies.

We have obtained the exclusive endorsement of six associations, and we market to their members. We also market locally to personal and commercial lines using ZIPDRIP, direct mail, and newsletters.

Tell me about your experience with QC/IPS.

I attended boot camp in 2006 and was in the top 12 in 2007. I also attended most of the fast start and closed door sessions.

The best part for me was meeting other members and taking part in an accountability group. It has also been helpful to hear the techniques being taught at each event.

Last year our revenue was up 23% and our volume increased 1.7 million.

What specific marketing advice or strategies would you give to another agent?

I would advise a new agent to attend events, join an accountability group and enter the Best Year Ever contest.

Why is this your Best Year Ever?

I have improved my business, improved my personal life, and spend more time away from the office. This has been a great year, and I plan for next year to be even better.

Jimmy McElreath's Secret Weapons

Jimmy took his cue from QC, developing an in-house competition, partnering with charities, and segmenting his client base. The tactics have worked beautifully-so we thought we should feature some here.

Create A Contest. Having seen the success of Quantum's Best Year Ever competition, Jimmy and his team decided to implement their own motivational contest.

The ATM's contest consisted of four elements: accountability, time, marketing and success. ATM's produce money, and Jimmy wanted to drive his employees to produce money.

Jimmy's employees kept binders to track their progress. For the Accountability section, employees had to list how they held themselves accountable during the week, to see what worked and how they stayed on track.

Employees also kept hourly, daily, and weekly logs to help them evaluate their time management and organize projects.

The Marketing portion of the contest allowed employees to contribute to the agency's marketing plans and goals, and the Success section was a chance for employees to exhibit their personal accomplishments within the agency.

Advertise with Community Benefits. Jimmy and his team convinced Builders Mutual to insure all new Habitat for Humanity homes in the area at no cost to the agency, which allowed for plenty of name recognition and association with an incredible charity. Jimmy's agency was also featured in the local paper for distributing a coloring book to help educate children about smoke detectors and fire exit drills.

Demonstrate Customer Appreciation. Around Thanksgiving, Jimmy sends a thank you letter to his customers and invites them to stop by the office to pick up a candy bar. His team also rented a booth at the local home and garden show and handed out gift certificates to visitors.

Focus on Customer Nurturing and Specialization. Jimmy and his team divide customers into 'A, B, C and D' categories. The goal is to move B and C clients into the A category, and trim away the D clients, who don't contribute enough to be sustainable. Specialized customer surveys are used to evaluate clients.

Jimmy is also a believer in niche marketing. He encourages agents to look at their current clients to develop a specialization. Often, a trend will emerge. Develop a relationship and market to clients, but also approach associations and get endorsements.

Size Up the Competition. Jimmy attributes his agency's growth this year to several things, but workers' compensation significantly contributed. He believes he was able to use workers' compensation to build his business, because other agencies didn't present very much competition.

119

10 – Gordon Sorrel

After completing college and his military obligations in 1973, Gordon Sorrel went to work for a homebuilder in Houston, Texas. Two years later he started his own real estate company. Gordon got into the insurance business in 1977 to augment his income as a realtor. He found that insurance was his real love and in 1980 began his own agency in north Houston. In 1982, Gordon incorporated the agency as Texas Insurance & Financial Services, Inc. In 1985 he sold the agency, kept the name, and moved to El Campo, Texas to be better able to take care of his mother. Since then he has bought and sold a number of agencies, always with growth in mind.

Outside of the office Gordon runs a cattle ranch, which takes almost all of his spare time. He had wanted to be a rancher right after college, but the business couldn't support a family on its own. Insurance has allowed Gordon to do what he really enjoys, while still earning a very good living.

Gordon and his wife of 34 years, Marilynn, have two sons, Todd and Ty. One is involved in the Premium Finance business in Austin, Texas and the other is a mutual fund analyst with Northern Trust in Chicago.

Gordon dearly loves bass fishing and has built a number of lakes on his property for the purpose of having the best bass fishing in Texas. While he hasn't achieved that goal yet, the project remains an enjoyable pursuit. The lakes also make for a great place to duck hunt when the weather is too cold to fish.

Gordon has a happy and comfortable life, thanks to years of hard work and the implementation of Quantum Club™ tools. He values his team, appreciates his customers, and has learned how to make the business work for him.

Where did you first learn about Insurance Profit Systems, Inc. and the Quantum Club™?

My office manager brought Insurance Profit Systems to my attention when she attended an IRS-AIMS Users Group meeting and met Mike Stromsoe. Mike was so excited about the potential that I couldn't help but be excited too.

What inspired you to try this program?

My inspiration was Mike Stromsoe. His enthusiasm was contagious.

What are you doing differently in your business?

Quantum Club™ has brought into focus some specific advertising techniques that I really hadn't thought of. As a result we are target marketing more than we already were. We had already been involved in niche marketing at the time we joined Quantum Club™, but QC gave us a better grip on how to do it more effectively.

What do you see as your "job"? What role do you play in your company?

My role in the agency has not changed that much, but the work that I do has changed greatly as a result of Quantum Club™. I still put in a full work week because I enjoy it so much, but now I am designing advertising game plans and continuously "tweaking" my vision of the agency as opportunities present themselves. The agency will grow not only by organic growth, but also by acquisition. That is a real challenge as the logistics of making an agency purchase work can be monumental.

Talk to me about your specific marketing strategies.

My specific marketing strategies revolve around the niche markets we have developed: wholesale nurseries, non-profit organizations, and beekeepers. For example, we knew that for the most part wholesale nurseries couldn't afford workers compensation insurance. Our competition dove head first into a workers' compensation program for the industry. We chose a different tact and recruited some companies to align with us and offer a non-subscriber program that would cover the same risks, but with a savings of 20-30%.

The program is still in the developmental stages, but it appears that this program is going to skunk the competition and give us a significant market edge for the other lines of business. These types of "out of the box" programs require a great deal of thought and coordination with companies and producers. Although these programs can be very time consuming, they are also quite rewarding.

Have you attended any of the IPS/QC boot camps, workshops, or other private sessions?

I attended the Closed Door session in San Diego in 2006, the Boot Camps in 2006 and 2007, and the niche marketing conference in 2007. I also sent one of my producers to the Personal Lines Conference in 2007.

Learning how other agents were approaching advertising and how Michael Jans was structuring an advertising program was very inspiring.

The agency is definitely more focused and the staff has more specific jobs and goals to achieve now than before.

How has your personal life improved since joining IPS/QC?

My priorities haven't changed since joining Quantum Club™. I still put in a full 40 hour week because I love it. If I were to take a vacation I can't think of doing anything more fun than working at the agency.

At the same time, I fully recognize my responsibilities to my family and the community I live in. Therefore, I balance my time between all of those things. I take stewardship of time and responsibility very seriously and always have. Quantum Club™ hasn't changed that.

What specific marketing advice or strategies would you give to another agent?

The best way to develop a successful marketing strategy is to stop thinking like an agent and begin thinking like a consumer.

Why is this your Best Year Ever?

This is my Best Year Ever because I became more focused, I see problems more clearly, and I have learned to see opportunities that I otherwise would have missed. The result was more profit and a more efficiently run agency. While we are not yet where we want to be, we are a long way ahead of where we were.

Gordon Sorrel's Secret Weapons

The client comes first. Most agents have heard this business motto, but Gordon and his team believe whole-heartedly in the concept. By putting the client first, Gordon is able to meet the needs of every member in every niche. He's also a proponent of self-analysis. He evaluates himself and his team regularly to assess progress and make sure the business runs effectively. Here are Gordon's best strategies.

Use Niche Marketing. If you rank your clients, you have already established niches for your agency. Market to a specific group of people-whether they are categorized by trade, economic status, premium, or any other criteria. Spending money on blanket advertising is wasteful; niche marketing concentrates your dollars on the clients who are most likely to buy.

Stand Out. One of Gordon's marketing tools is a tradeshow or convention survival kit. Tradeshow visitors enjoy the funny kits, which break the monotony. Now people ask Gordon's team for the kits, which have become a trademark. Come up with a niche-specific give-away that will impress clients and help your agency stand out.

Do What's Best for the Client. Resolve all office disputes by doing what's best for the client. Everything else is secondary.

Identify and Eliminate Weakness. Gordon recommends the Five Dysfunctions of a Team **by** Patrick Lencioni. Figuring out what can tear your team apart is crucial. Identifying and fixing weaknesses early will help you develop the most effective team.

SAMPLE

TEXAS INSURANCE &
FINANCIAL SERVICES, INC.

Trusted
Choice™

Given to both clients and prospects when attending a niche mkt. trade show.

Thank you for participating in our Mystery Shopper program. Texas Insurance & Financial Services and Traditions Insurance Services are committed to providing superior customer service and exceptional products. Our clients deserve to receive outstanding customer service from their insurance companies and our agency. This program will help our Insurance Protection Team to continue to work even better for you.

For participating in our Mystery Shopper program
you will receive a $25 gift card.

It is this simple:

★ Call 800-541-9849 and request a free, no obligation quote

Worker's Comp	**Property**	**Life & Health**
Nursery Stock	**Crop Insurance**	

★ Judge the service, knowledge and price

★ Send us your Mystery Shopper information

★ We send you $25 American Express Gift Certificate

Attached is the Mystery Shopper form for judging the call and a pre-paid envelope.

Again thank you for your participation and we look forward to receiving your remarks.

102 N. WASHINGTON • P.O. BOX 950 • EL CAMPO, TEXAS 77437
(979) 543-2709 • FAX (979) 543-9030 • EMAIL: txins@txins.com • WEBSITE: www.txins.com

128

11 – Rob Zabbia

THE DIRTY DOZEN DIARIES

"… nothing is more beneficial than getting to talk to other agents who have already been through what you are experiencing …!"

-ROB ZABBIA

For Rob Zabbia, the insurance business is a family affair. He started working in college, taking a job in an auto parts store. After graduation Rob parlayed his experience into a position selling information management systems to auto parts stores. After six years, his father finally managed to convince Rob to work with him in the insurance business, with the plan that Rob would eventually take over the agency.

After a year, Allstate appointed Rob as an agent, but he continued to work in the same office as his dad. They merged the two agencies almost five years ago. The rest is history.

While Rob is fortunate to work with family, he enjoys spending time outside of work with family even more. Because his mother was one of six children, Rob has lots of close cousins. He grew up with an appreciation for quality time with family. He and his wife have four year old twins, Daniel and Jessica, and Rob spends every moment he can with them. He believes in engaging his children in developmental activities like swimming, karate, and dancing.

Rob personally enjoys classic cars, and loves to take his son along to car shows. (He's especially fond of the 1968 mustang that his dad bought for him.) His daughter, however, is very much a girly-girl, and prefers American Girl dolls and princesses to hot rods. So the family often gets roped into doing those types of activities, too.

Thanks to the tips and techniques he learned in Quantum Club™, Rob is able to spend even more time with his family. Before the twins were born, Rob and his wife were avid skiers, and took several trips a year. Now that the twins are old enough, the family takes an annual ski vacation. Rob Zabbia is living proof that with the right strategies and clear goals, work and family mix quite well.

Where did you first learn about Insurance Profit Systems, Inc. and the Quantum Club™?

I received several letters from Michael about QC, but disregarded them because I had a successful agency.

But then the market changed, and things were going on around and within the industry that were out of my control. I had essentially taken my business as far as I could on my own.

I learned about a free conference with John Mason. I knew of John from my involvement in the industry, so I hopped on the call. After hearing what he had to say, I signed up.

What inspired you to try this program?

The call inspired me. I was searching for something. I'd been through a lot of training with Allstate, and I'd always heard that agents should work on the agency rather than in the agency. Everyone always said that, but never fully explained what was meant.

I could tell that was what QC was all about. I would finally learn the secret of how to work on, not in, my agency.

What are you doing differently in your business?

We now have a team. Before there was only so much of me to go around. Now, I can get my staff to sell better and work toward our goals.

What do you see as your "job"? What role do you play in your company?

I'm the strategic planner. Basically, I'm the one who dives in deep to find out what we need to do. I am able to succeed by using what I learned in QC, Michael's tools, my own experience, and my dad's experience. I put all of that together to take us to the next phase.

Now we set more goals, and we communicate better than before. I develop, implement, and manage a plan, rather than getting on the phone to close a bunch of deals so we can make our numbers.

Tell me about your experience with QC/IPS.

I've been to both boot camps since I joined, and every one of the Closed Door Sessions except two. The only reason I missed any at all was because I had other obligations.

FAST STATS

Years In IPS/QC:
3
Hours Per Week:
40-45
Total Staff:
13

This year I'll be at every event. They are already on my calendar.

The cumulative knowledge has got to be the best part. We start using what Michael teaches and shares with us right away. And nothing is more beneficial than getting to talk to other agents who have already been through what you are experiencing. I get to see what's working for other agents and tweak their methods so they work for my market. We learn to just keep trying things until they work.

We've grown about 20%. I purchased another agency, and was still able to cut my work week down by about five hours.

Before QC I never would have thought about buying another agency, because that's more work that I have to do. Thanks to QC techniques, I only spend four hours a week in the other agency, which has also grown about 20%.

How has your personal life improved since joining IPS/QC?

I drive my kids to school two days a week, and I'm not stuck at the office until seven every night. I don't have to work on the weekends, and we very rarely have a night appointment.

I also have more time to travel. I used to dread vacations because I'd have so much work when I got back. I would come in very early to catch up on the work. I was pressured to make more sales to make up for time when I was gone. Now when I come back the desk is actually cleaner than when I left.

Why is this your Best Year Ever?

I was able to buy another agency, and not have to be there all of the time. That never would have happened without everything that I've learned over the past three years. The important thing is to step away from your business and figure out how to make everything work without you being there. A lot of insurance agents do that, but they aren't able to grow at the same time. QC teaches you how to do both.

Rob Zabbia's Secret Weapons

Rob teaches us that working with what you have can be very productive. He believes in team motivation and relying on his current client base to help grow his business. The following tips elaborate on those strategies, along with advice about organization and stacked marketing campaigns.

Use Repetition. Focus on selling as many policies as possible to existing clients. Add several new campaigns to the marketing plan every year. For example, sell homeowners policies to people with an auto policy, etc.

Selling as much as you possibly can to each client is better than trying to bring in more households. Managing 10,000 policies for 5,000 people is easier than handling 10,000 for 10,000 people.

Search Your Existing Client Base for Leads. Look for new clients by reviewing where you found your old clients. Don't just buy a list; choose targets based on your current clients' industries, neighborhoods, etc.

Supercharge the Team. If you want to get big, get your staff on board. Rob pays low salaries, but offers commission and bonuses for all sales. The cost of providing employee incentives is minimal compared to the growth in revenue generated by a passionate team.

Get Organized. Rob says he is successful, because he took the time to "get his house in order." Time management is essential, and so is having a clear plan and set of objectives for each member of the team. Rob recommends a full time assistant that can help manage the staff.

Rob also carefully plans his marketing campaigns (in detail) ahead of time.

Use Scripts. You may not think this step is necessary, but Rob swears his team is more successful now that they know exactly what to say. Up-selling will increase, but only if your staff is supercharged and open to the technique.

Be Proactive. Rob's team does not wait for calls; calling prospects (at least twenty a day) is part of the daily schedule.

12 – Joel Zwicker

Joel began his career in the golf industry. For ten years, he worked in various positions, from club scrubber to assistant manager and apprentice professional. After high school, he attended Acadia University in Wolfville, Nova Scotia and earned a business degree.

After college, the golf industry wasn't exactly paying the bills, so Joel took some advice from a friend of the family and began working in the insurance industry as an adviser for SunLife Financial. After 6 months of starving, he was contemplating going back to the golf course for the summer. Then, a woman from A.A. Munro Insurance called and asked Joel if he was interested in a position at a new office the company was opening in the area.

Initially, Joel declined because he thought he'd had as much of the insurance industry as he could handle. But he later agreed to meet the owner of the company, Harley, and as they say, the rest is history!

Joel says, "I couldn't ask for a better life outside of the office. I have a beautiful family." Joel and his wife Natasha have two children, Caleb and Sarah. They live in a small village about ten minutes from the office.

Joel's family is what drives him to succeed. Though he didn't grow up poor, Joel still wants his children to have a better life than he did. His goal is to provide for them in such a manner that they will never have any worries as long as they live. According to the results he demonstrated to our judges, Joel is well on his way to achieving that goal.

Where did you first learn about Insurance Profit Systems, Inc. and the Quantum Club™?

After we opened the office in New Minas, we really struggled for the first 6 or 7 months and did very little business. One afternoon, we had a meeting with Harley. He brought a box of stuff from Insurance Profit Systems – a Boot Camp in a Box from 2004 or 2005 – and said, "Why don't we give this a shot?"

Harley left the box with us and arranged a tutorial of the Quantum Web site for me. I read over some of the materials and remember thinking, "This stuff is crazy, but what do we have to lose?" We weren't doing well doing things our way, so we decided to give it a try.

What inspired you to try this program?

As I said earlier, we had nothing to lose. In our first 7 months in New Minas, we had only written 114 policies. We were a sinking ship that had never gotten a chance to sail. Sometimes in life you cannot wait for your ship to come in, you gotta jump in and swim and that's what we did with IPS.

What are you doing differently in your business?

Everything. From the day-to-day operations to our marketing campaigns to the general atmosphere in the office, everything has changed since we started doing business the IPS way. We have definitely gone through some changes because of staffing. We had gotten so busy with just two of us in the office we actually had to make an attempt to get the phones to stop ringing. I had heard it said once that you had to get your house in order before you start marketing hard but I really didn't take that advice seriously until it was too late. So 4 months after stopping literally everything we had working for us it finally tamed down to the point where we could train some new staff to our way of thinking and get the ball rolling again. It was not easy for us to change things totally as A.A. Munro Insurance has 15 other offices in our province and really has great workflows and ways of doing business, but we were trying to make the change to the sales mentality which went against the flow, but it has all worked out and it's full throttle forward!

What do you see as your "job"? What role do you play in your company?

When I started with A.A. Munro, I was nothing more than an insurance broker that sat behind his desk, pushing home and auto policies. Now I'm an insurance marketer, which has become a prominent theme within the company.

A.A. Munro Insurance has 16 offices across Nova Scotia. The ideas that we implemented in our small, made from scratch agency have spread into those other offices with great success. Now I am the other offices' source for marketing ideas and campaigns. I currently only spend about 25% of my time doing 'insurance broker' type activities. The rest of the time I work on insurance marketing activities like campaigns, newsletters, cross-selling letters and niche marketing.

Talk to me about your specific marketing strategies.

Michael Jans preaches, "What is Marketing?" or "What is Insurance Marketing?" He says it is the "Attraction, Conversion, and Retention of clients at the highest long-term profit." I like that theory, and I believe in it. However, I also believe in branding to make yourself easier to remember – something catchy. A.A. Munro has great brand recognition in the Northeastern part of Nova Scotia. However, we are in the Southwest part of the province where no one has a clue as to who A.A. Munro Insurance is.

What we noticed when our marketing initially started to work was that people would come into our office and use the old adage, "We hear you folks got the sharpest pencil in town," so we started using the phrase ourselves and it really took off. So now, in everything we do in this office, we promote the brand, "Sharpest Pencil in Town." We are also in the process of starting another 'brand' for high-end personal line and commercial line clients called TIP (Total Insurance Protection) in hopes of attracting more of that business.

Tell me about your experience with QC/IPS.

Since joining IPS in early 2006 I have not missed a boot camp. I have also attended a Personal Lines Super Conference, and participated in as many of the conference calls as possible. You can sit in your office and read about the stuff that works for other people or what Michael believes will work for you all you want, but until you have the opportunity to attend a function and see and talk with the people that are actually using his ideas and the different twists they put on the concepts you really don't get the full value.

I can honestly say that I have never gone to an IPS event and not picked up a new idea that didn't pay for the event five times over within the first month. At the most recent Boot Camp, the Senior Vice President of A.A. Munro Insurance came with me and within the first hour of the event he was in absolute awe and had already begun thoughts of how to make changes company wide.

FAST STATS

Years In IPS/QC:
2
Hours Per Week:
30 - 40
Total Staff:
5

Michael Jans is a phenomenal speaker. His ideas will change the way you look at your business forever. The presentations, the top notch guest speakers he attracts, and the other agents that speak are worth every penny. That's where you get your best ideas: listening to real people tell real stories about things that have worked for them.

Being a member of IPS has meant the difference between being a profitable agency in just a year and a half and being an agency that might have taken 6 or 7 years to break even. In just two years, we went from having 2 of us in the office twiddling our thumbs most of the time to having 5 full-time staff – and we're likely hiring a sixth full-time staffer in the next 6 months. Using the techniques and ideas gained from these events, in the same short two year period we have become a force to be reckoned with, in our territory. Many of our larger competitors spend their sales meetings discussing how to compete or deal with the threat that comes from us.

How has your personal life improved since joining IPS/QC?

I have gone from 70 hour work weeks and selling policies in parking lots to a 40 hour work week – if that – and doing what I love: marketing and meeting people. I'm only 27 years old so there's no need to totally retire yet, but I do get to spend twice as much time with my children now. With that said I love to go to work now and play the game, because that is what it has become for me, a game. It's a game I'm winning at and I intend to dominate at!

What specific marketing advice or strategies would you give to another agent?

Just keep doing what you're doing and I'll keep eating your dinner right off of your plate. Truthfully, my advice is just do it. The biggest mistake people make is spending too much time on figuring out what they should do. Start something, track it, and if it doesn't work – try something else, I guess it's the old 80% rule!!

Mass Implementation + Mass Tracking & Evaluation + Mass Tinkering = Massive Growth

Why is this your Best Year Ever?

Well, 201% policy growth with 191% premium growth and 186% revenue growth with more time with family and a new cottage on the lake goes a long way. However, in the words of another Quantum member, this is my "Best Year Yet!"

Joel Zwicker's Secret Weapons

Joel prides himself on being able to think outside of the box. His marketing tactics are unexpected, original and effective. Following are tips derived from some of Joel's bold marketing choices.

Branding Works. A catchy slogan has helped establish Joel's agency as one of the most recognizable in the area. Consumers remember the agency name when they are looking for insurance. You don't have to be talking insurance but when someone asks or makes reference to 'The Sharpest Pencil in Town' the conversation immediately turns to Joel Zwicker and A.A. Munro Insurance.

Referrals are Currency. Joel offers standard homeowners insurance policies to mini-home owners at a deep discount. Joel combats doubtful agents with this: "There are two ways to make a million in life. You can sell one thing at a million or you can sell a million things at a buck, and I love the referrals that come from those million people."

Detailed Testmonials. Prospects are more willing to trust the recommendations of people they know. Under the name of each testimonial, include the city or neighborhood. Prospects in those areas will trust a testimonial from their own neighborhood.

Yard Signs. Like contractors and real estate agents, Joel asks permission from his clients to put out a yard sign. People driving by see the brand, the number, and call for a free quote. Joel considers this his best idea - one that has huge results!

FaceBook. Create a webpage for your clients to visit and network. People who visit social networking sites are religious users. Give prospects a place to learn about your company and the benefits of becoming a client.

13 – Bill Gough

Bill Gough started with Allstate at age 24. That was his first job after graduation, and he's still working there today.

Bill will admit that he was a tough sell when it came to Quantum Club. Eventually, his reluctance gave way to his curiosity. After only one Boot Camp, Bill decided QC has plenty to offer.

Now Bill is more successful than ever before. And he credits his QC tools and the network of experienced agents with his progress. Bill believes that if he can make these strategies work for himself, anyone can be successful.

Bill's primary motivation is his family. His success as an agent allows him plenty of free time to do the activities he enjoys most: golf and travel. He also has a great time on international trips with Allstate.

Where did you first learn about Insurance Profit Systems, Inc. and the Quantum Club?

I first learned about IPS four years ago. At first, I ignored the direct mail for several years, but Michael was persistent. Then my friend, David Spence, a Quantum Club member, insisted Michael Jans had something to offer me. He said, "You've just got to do this. You're going to love it. I know you. You're going to love it." I took his advice, and he was so right.

What inspired you to try this program?

Michael's persistence and David Spence's recommendation.

What are you doing differently in your business?

I was already doing well on my own, but Quantum Club showed me how to focus on what was most important. QC has also allowed me more time off and taught me to empower my employees.
Tell me about your experience with QC/IPS.

I've been to four boot camps in a row. My first meeting was actually the 2004 boot camp. I only knew two people there and was very skeptical. In fact, I was pretty determined not to buy into any of Jans' stuff, yet the more I saw, the more I was convinced. The networking is invaluable.

FAST STATS

Years In IPS/QC:
4
Hours Per Week:
8 – 10 in the office
12 – 16 at home
Total Staff:
12

What specific marketing advice or strategies would you give to another agent?

Measure your new business production – such as where your new business sources come from, what you're spending on leads, and your output. We call our measurement system the New Business Production Log.

Why is this your Best Year Ever?

We have contributed $19,000 to the scholarship fund and the American Diabetes association, and our client referrals are up by 600%.

Bill Gough's Secret Weapons

Like all members of the Dirty Dozen, Bill has demonstrated excellence in marketing. He nurtures his team, hires effectively, and goes out of his way to thank his clients. Here are the specifics of Bill's best tactics.

Client Appreciation Events. Bill plans large dinners or other events, which usually include a seminar, for his clients. Referrals are easily generated if you make your clients happy.

End of Year VIP Mailers. Annual reports about new programs, contest winners, and charity funds are always successful. Clients especially appreciate knowing how their dollars were contributed to charity.

Hire Slow, Fire Fast. Employees are a reflection of you and your agency. For them to work well, they must fit the right profile. Take the time to really consider employees before hiring. Profile every applicant you are seriously considering. And trim the fat. Employees have to be empowered. They must be self-motivators who want to be on the team. If they aren't- they're out.

Nurture the Team. Nurturing clients is important, but many staff members spend more time at work than they do with their own families. Create a positive, rewarding environment to inspire employees. Work can be fun.

Conclusion

The thirteen agents introduced in this book were chosen for several reasons. They are considered exemplary in their level of success, and are outstanding in their commitment to the core values of Quantum Club™. These agents don't set the standards, they exceed expectations. Their agencies are proof of the effectiveness of Quantum Club™ techniques and tools. Consider the common benefits expressed by every member of the Dirty Dozen:

- ✓ Less time in the office
- ✓ More effective staff
- ✓ Tremendous growth
- ✓ Better office efficiency
- ✓ Increased profits

Because all Quantum Club™ members possess the tools to become exceptional business people, these agents get credit for being the best of the best.

Quantum Club™ began because I had a vision of what the insurance industry could be. I am proud to say that, one QC member at a time; we are changing the face of the industry.

Innovation is worthless if new concepts aren't embraced by the business community. Quantum

Club™ has been successful because the members have welcomed my methods with open arms. They enthusiastically implement new strategies and challenge me to raise the bar every year. Thanks to every agent who has joined in the revolution. Congratulations for having the courage to transform your businesses, and your lives.